RETIRE WITH

a Mission

★

Planning and Purpose for the Second Half of Life

Richard G. Wendel, MD, MBA

SOURCEBOOKS, INC.®
NAPERVILLE, ILLINOIS

Copyright © 2008 by Richard G. Wendel
Cover and internal design © 2008 by Sourcebooks, Inc.
Cover photos © iStockphoto.com / Skip O'Donnell, Catherine Yeulet
Cover design by KT Design

Published by Sourcebooks, Inc.
P.O. Box 4410, Naperville, Illinois 60567-4410
(630) 961-3900
Fax: (630) 961-2168
www.sourcebooks.com

Library of Congress Cataloging-in-Publication Data

Wendel, Richard G.

  Retire with a mission : planning and purpose for the second half of life / Richard G. Wendel.

       p. cm.

  Includes bibliographical references and index.

  1. Retirement. 2. Retirement--Planning. 3. Older people--Conduct of life. 4. Quality of life. I. Title.

  HQ1062.W45 2008

  646.7'9--dc22

2008027160

Printed and bound in the United States of America.
VP 10 9 8 7 6 5 4 3 2 1

Dedication

Dedicated to my wife, Ann, as a tribute to her adjustment to my retirement.

Contents

Acknowledgments

The author is indebted to many colleagues and friends for encouragement and creative ideas to improve the manuscript. Dr. Roy Whitman, a professor of psychiatry at the University of Cincinnati College of Medicine, reviewed the psychological content of Section II. Lewis Gatch, an attorney, composed Chapter 12, "The Skinny on Estate Planning." I offer special thanks to Colleen Glenn, Dawn Ramirez, and Anne Bowling for their assistance in the editing process.

Introduction

YOUR NEWFOUND FREEDOM

Gainful employment places the clock squarely in the center of your universe. Usually the occupation you have chosen channels your best energies and ideas toward satisfying the goals and objectives of the firm. Customers must be satisfied, bosses placated, and company culture adhered to. Other people gauge your productivity, and the firm defines and shapes your aspirations. A facade of interactive congeniality, cooperation, and teamwork is necessary to perform the job.

During the working years the routines of the workplace are generally given precedence over all other activities. Home, family life, and enjoyable pastimes ordinarily take a back seat to work commitments. Consequently, work often siphons your most creative energies and carries a high opportunity cost that prohibits other forms of self-expression. Employment begs the question: Who needs these hassles that place you on a treadmill, in a box, and under the gun of performance?

Despite the pervasive publicity about stress management, most individuals don't fully appreciate how stressful their jobs were until they retire and look back. And this observation spans all gender, ethnic, and employment differences. Indeed, retrospect leads many to realize that they were living that well-known "life of quiet desperation."

Retirement is an incredibly good time to enjoy life. The two foremost luxuries of retirement are less stress and an adaptable schedule. To phrase it differently, in retirement you have the empowerment to ignore the metronome of the clock and the discretion to control your schedule. Further, to put it in childhood terms, you can generally do what you want to do, when you want to do it.

You have the freedom to let your personal interests take center stage. Your activities are no longer measured by profitability, but by self-satisfaction. You can pick and choose with whom you wish to associate. The previous overriding competition between work and play ceases when you cross the threshold of retirement.

Freedom from the rigors of gainful employment makes time for satisfying pastimes. Retirement facilitates a focus on a healthy lifestyle with regular exercise and ample rest. The windfall of time and energy can be redirected to spouses, grandchildren, hobbies, travel, sports, reading, gardening, and so on. Retirement offers a surefire prescription to achieve stress-free living.

However, there is no rulebook, no standards, and no explicit training manual for retirement. Without exception, it takes time and patience to reengineer the business behaviors and expectations of a lifetime into a new context—a new mission. And this new mission is highlighted by self-direction, self-sufficiency, and self-satisfaction that make for a breathtaking journey in retirement.

THE END OF AN ERA

There are seventy-three million baby-boomers—with a net worth of about $25 trillion—reaching retirement age over the next decade. This diffusion of wealth has fostered a realistic goal of early retirement. Indeed, a recent AARP survey revealed that when a random group was asked at what age they wanted to stop working entirely for pay, the average age was 59.7 years. And when asked at what age they expected to stop working for pay, the answer was 63.7 years.

Today, a retirement party just a few years after the sentinel fiftieth birthday is commonplace. To compound this demographic shift to early retirement, life expectancy for both men and women is dramatically increasing the period of highly functional life beyond the retirement age. On average, today a sixty-five-year-old can expect to live sixteen to twenty more years and an eighty-five-year-old seven more years.

This poses a genuine paradox: While advancements in healthcare and healthy lifestyles improve quality and length of life, at the same time social trends embrace the early escape from the rigors of full-time employment. If this trend continues and is exacerbated by a declining numbers of younger workers, who is going to pay the Social Security and pension benefits for this large group of retired persons to live on? Estimates vary, but the Office of the Actuary gives an unfunded pension liability figure for America of about $10.5 trillion, and experts from the American Enterprise Institute estimate unfunded liabilities for Medicare at about $36.6 trillion. These are sums that vastly exceed the current GDP of about $13 trillion. At some point in time, our elected representatives must bite the bullet and craft the painful, necessary solutions.

Whatever the financial underpinnings, your retirement will not be a static end point for demobilization, but rather an opportunity for new beginnings. Retirement leverages the rewards of a productive career to focus on a new rainbow of possibilities. This is especially true since you come equipped with a lifetime of experience and preferences, both excellent drawing tools that can help you create a new blueprint for this liberated stage of life.

Historical Perspective

Political, social, and financial factors have all contributed to the drive toward early retirement in the twentieth and twenty-first centuries. Before WWII, retirement was uncommon without a precipitating factor such as disability, debility, or senility. In 1950, the average retiree lived just 1.5 years following retirement. But in the last half of the twentieth century, unprecedented prosperity and wealth accumulation caused social and cultural norms to change. Retirement became a realistic expectation. The federal government obligingly enacted Social Security and Medicare, and fostered wealth accumulation via pension and profit-sharing plans, 401(k) plans, and other tax-deferred savings vehicles. The plans provide a secure financial base for a large segment of the populace approaching retirement. This security has given today's retiree a wide range of options.

The Changing Workplace

Marketplace forces have changed the way our nation does business—rapid technological change, cutthroat competition, and an obsession with the bottom line have corralled the energies of the boardroom and senior management. Corporate strategy and business planning are more focused on the survival and growth of the company than the employees, and often, business decisions supersede the interests of the ordinary worker. Employers look for flexibility within the labor markets and adjust their workforces to meet fluctuations in demand, while still capturing productivity gains to "right size" their workforces. In response to supply and demand, temporary workers (or temps) are frequently used to ramp up or ramp down production.

The company paternalism and loyalty to the worker that was a hallmark of small business early in the twentieth century has faded. In response, the workforce has had to become resilient by learning new skills when migrating between jobs and ascending the corporate ladder. Often a job is considered an addition to the curriculum vitae and a career-enhancing step along the way to the next job. The model of working at one job until retirement has changed drastically. Having a variety of career experiences may afford a degree of adaptability, but it often precludes the forming of close bonds between employer and employee, and takes away the option to gradually transition into retirement.

The new business vocabulary is riddled with ominous terms like "downsizing," "reorganization," "layoffs," "outsourcing," "merger," "acquisition," "strategic partnerships," "virtual enterprises," and "joint ventures." These events that pare and reshuffle the workforce must be considered drivers of premature and early retirement, both voluntary and involuntary. Generous severance packages, golden parachutes (a clause in an executive's contract that promises stock options, severance, etc., in the case of termination), and rich benefits for attrition-based downsizing add to the ranks of early retirees. The new economy espouses free trade, globalization, and shareholder value, terms that mean little to the employee aside from a threat of lower wages and displacement.

In addition, the workplace is more demanding of today's worker.

New, complex technology, productivity standards, and continuous quality improvement have pushed the envelope of endurance and stress tolerance. A maze of arbitrary regulations and mandated accountability produce a mountain of paperwork. The typical hassle factors in our rapidly paced society make retirement look like Nirvana. It is not surprising that surveys consistently show that one in five people say they want to retire as early as possible.

A SMOOTH TRANSITION

Research has shown a correlation between happiness in retirement and certain broad parameters. In general, the more social, intellectual, and financial resources brought to retirement, the smoother the adjustment. A solid marriage, high degree of education, broad circle of friends, and respected "body of work" during one's career are especially valuable assets heading into retirement. From a more general perspective, the more control you have enjoyed over the silos of your life, the easier the transition.

Studies have also shown that being affluent and well educated carries a healthy survival benefit or longevity bonus of about five years. The English Longitudinal Study of Aging (ELSA) in Britain suggests that being on the top of the heap postpones the onset of mental and physical disability by about fifteen years compared to those in lower socioeconomic groups.

The time needed to settle into the leisure routines of retirement is usually longer for younger retirees. They have fewer peers with whom to share the experience, and society tacitly frowns on what may be considered premature retirement. For single individuals with weak family or companionship ties, retirement may often be accompanied by a period of increased loneliness and isolation. This is especially true if the job left behind was meaningful and well compensated. The reason for retirement is also important. If the retiree wants to retire and it is a voluntary act—rather than an involuntary occurrence—it produces a more positive attitude with less emotional fallout.

New Horizons

Today a friendly and vibrant culture characterizes the retirement community. Like marriage and the fortieth birthday, retirement conjures up a repertoire of tongue-in-cheek expressions that poke fun and delight. Retirement ceremonies are much more elaborate than just receiving the gold pocket watch for thirty years of service. At the end of the celebrations at home and at work, the retiree graduates into the 10-percent-AARP-discount culture designed to maintain the buying habits of the now fixed-income buyers.

The retiree has an unlimited range of captivating diversions. Travel destinations abound that suit any taste, special interest, or level of risky behavior. Transportation to most any place on Earth can easily be booked. Communication technology makes staying in touch effortless. Museums for almost any discipline, social phenomenon, science, cultural trend, historical period, sport, and pop trend dot the landscapes of our great cities. The performing arts and sports are alive in our metropolitan areas, and infinite opportunities exist to volunteer for worthy causes in our communities.

Segments of residential construction have been transformed to serve the needs of empty-nesters, retirees, and elders. Homes and condo complexes often have fewer bedrooms with small but deluxe kitchens, and a room to accommodate a home office. Ranch-style floor plans with wider doorways to accommodate wheelchairs and bathrooms with grab bars are frequent design features. Large condo complexes are tiered with large decks and covered balconies that provide a pleasant ambience for reading and enjoying the view. The larger developments provide shuttle services, and most have easy access to public transportation. And a comfortable, country-club atmosphere of activity and socializing is an integral part of retirement living centers.

Retirees flock to the southern United States to enjoy a warmer climate that permits outdoor "sweater" activity even in the depths of winter. They often become permanent residents, or "snow birds," who gather to build stable communities that mirror those they left in the North. Many retirement communities are gated and offer tight security. The larger ones often mimic small municipalities with police and fire services, a gift shop and general store, meeting and dining facilities, golf course and tennis courts, and so on. And almost all retirement settlements are located close to communities with low crime rates; an active, clean, and safe downtown; and a good hospital. Many periodicals, such as the magazine *Where to Retire,* are devoted to helping the retiree select the ultimate retirement home.

It's easy to see why retirement has such a powerful magnetism.

Letting Go of the Old to Set the Stage for the New

Retirement is an opportune time in life to let go of unfulfilled dreams and emotional conflict. At the end of the day, retirement makes unmet, lofty career aspirations moot; why not accept the reality, and purge them from your narrative? Feuds with coworkers, maintaining status in the workplace, and work grievances are no longer relevant; clear the slate and leave them behind. The tether of employment that puts you in a box has vanished, and the doors are open to your own brand of creativity. Enjoy the freedom and carefree acceptance outside of the business world, much the same way you may have enjoyed the power and status attendant to gainful employment. Inevitably, the old order yields to the new. Facilitate and accept the transition—don't resist it. Rejoice that the competition has come to an end; just because you no longer compete against others for accolades doesn't mean you won't be striving to be the best.

Goals that are tempered by a lifetime of experience are usually very realistic. With ordinary living comes the insight that no one has infinite wisdom or special knowledge to make a perfect world. Few issues in life are either black or white, and virtually all ethical dilemmas defy resolution. Acknowledge and accept this as the human state. Then accept your uniqueness and limitations. Retirement is a time to go with the flow, let your hair down, and relax.

Changing Patterns from the Past

Many people boast that they'll make radical changes in retirement. However, most of us tend to stick to the patterns that have served us well. Covertly, we are all creatures of habit. Everyone has a history and memories both pleasant and unpleasant that subsume his or her behavior. Life will always produce tensions between freedom and rootedness, adventure and security, and family responsibility and personal fulfillment. In addition, every choice will continue to have an opportunity cost that displaces other alternatives. The very nature of retirement requires a realignment of activities to provide new meaning and purpose.

With advancing age, it is a generally accepted belief that individuals become more rigid in their viewpoints and resistant to new ideas. Indeed, the journey of life does temper your worldview. In addition, seniority and experience give you the credentials and poetic license to express your true feelings. Often, belief systems and innate character become more transparent. This explains some of the perceived diversity seen in senior citizens, who at times are more unlike one another than even adolescents.

This book is constructed as an upbeat practical guide to the retirement experience. There is a special emphasis on psychology, family matters, health and sexual functioning, possession and money management, and getting prepared. The book strives to provide the framework to understand retirement and clearly outline the strategies to embrace its inherent magic, adventure, fun, fulfillment, and creative expression. And in the process of planning, you will develop a unique and personal mission statement to guide your way.

SECTION 1:

Preparation

CHAPTER 1

Creating the Foundation
for a Smooth Transition

*C*onversations between people approaching retirement often follow along these lines: "I'm not sure what I'll do when I retire, and I'm too busy now to even think about it." Paying your children's college tuition, home mortgages, catastrophic medical expenses, and other obligations may push any thought of retirement far into the future. Other people procrastinate because they think they have too few outside interests such as athletics, travel, and hobbies to keep themselves occupied. Some have an addiction to the work routine or a stressful home environment that keeps them from calling it quits so they can still get out of the house every day. And some have the need to retain the power and discretionary spending that gainful employment provides. Thus, plans for retirement often remain vague and only marginally thought out. This lack of planning might catch you off guard if you're forced to retire due to an unanticipated career interruption such as failing health, business failures, enterprise downsizing, layoffs due to outsourcing and mergers, and so on.

With so many variables it is not surprising that most people stumble into retirement with little or no forethought. But planning for retirement is very worthwhile. The earlier you start, the greater the chances are of finding out what makes you genuinely happy, and creating the infrastructure and environment to pursue your own special Camelot for the retirement years.

EXPECTATIONS VS. REALITY

High Expectations

To some, the word retirement conjures up an image of wide-open pastures with cows grazing on lush grass under a sunny sky. Some people think of retirement as a one-way ticket to utopia, an immediate relief from onerous work and stressful demands. Still others may characterize retirement as a return to a carefree childhood or, perhaps, expect the exhilaration of finishing a marathon, reaching the peak of the mountain, or receiving the trophy for winning the tournament. For a CEO, it might be akin to being kicked upstairs to the position as chairman of the board.

Retirement comes with high expectations. Indeed retirement offers many immediate pleasures. Who can object to a flexible schedule with no deadlines and uncluttered time? Or relief from supervision and reporting to your superiors at the firm? And every day is a holiday?

The Reality

Each of us brings a complete set of circumstances to the threshold of retirement. Our personalities don't dramatically change, the family does not suddenly come together, your golf handicap probably won't change, and personal assets will not increase unless you have a golden parachute, stock options, or deferred compensation from your place of employment. What retirement does do is give you a "time out" in which to reinvent yourself. Remember that retirement has no standard rulebook to follow; you must create your own blueprint or roadmap. It is not surprising that this momentous change in orientation from the routines of work to the amorphous luxury of self-direction can be disconcerting. With ambiguity always comes some measure of ambivalence.

With ambiguity always comes some measure of ambivalence.

In reality, the early years of retirement are often a turbulent stretch in life's journey. Perhaps more than any other period in life, this milestone pushes your envelope of social change and personal adjustment. Your schedule of daily activities is scrambled. New roles and relationships alter the landscape and muddy the comfort zone of familiarity. The changing of the guard often carries with it the message of "you are a has-been" that may threaten your identity and feelings of self-esteem. Plus, the retirement years coincide with the downward slope of mental and physical capabilities. And this challenge must be coupled with the residual feelings of loss from leaving your friends at the workplace behind, surrendering your position to someone new (and likely, younger), and losing your paycheck.

The emotional adjustment to retirement takes time, and each retiree settles in at a different rate. On average, several years are required to achieve a satisfactory new equilibrium and comfort level.

You must be patient during this natural transition period and give yourself the slack to flounder and backslide from time to time.

WHY YOU SHOULD PLAN

A straw poll of thirty prospective retirees showed that few had critically reviewed all major retirement issues. In many instances, financial needs were projected using fuzzy math and rosy assumptions. Virtually no one realized that spending usually increases during the two years following retirement, in part due to greater travel expense, more meals at local restaurants, do-it-yourself home repairs, and the trappings of renewed and broadened interest in new hobbies. The impact upon spouses and family was often considered a side issue, even though retirement has a profound effect on all household relationships. And most overestimated their physical capability to sustain a daily diet of strenuous physical activities such as golf, remodeling, camping, gardening, and coaching Little League baseball. After discussing the results, most acknowledged that diligent planning would have smoothed the transition and helped prevent nasty surprises.

However, retirement shouldn't start with a full dance card. You should be able to make up the program as it goes along—that's a major part of the fun and the poetic license that retirement permits. When retirement arrives, everyone wants to know how you plan to keep busy. This obsession with engagement is ingrained in the American-cultural work ethic; idleness is equated with laziness. Thus, you may feel compelled to pad and embellish your alleged plans long before they have been thought through.

Retirement is far from a static state; it is a continuum of change. Patience is a great virtue in navigating the change. Margery Williams's Skin Horse in *The Velveteen Rabbit* says, "It doesn't happen all at once—you become." Positive and confident attitudes smooth the way—just hold tight to the belief that you'll overcome the challenges.

Before the big day arrives, there are some constructive steps and a change in social orientation that can help you to proactively prepare for your needs in retirement.

1. Developing a Network of Friends: The Differences between Men and Women

Independence, stoicism, and self-sufficiency are valued traits amongst the alpha males/hunters in our culture. Due to these real or imagined societal norms, men become more focused on competition than cooperation and collaboration. They are generally good negotiators but are generally less skilled at maintaining and nurturing relationships than women. As a result, men often have few close friends and real confidants. Moreover, with those whom they would call close friends, they often bond through common interests such as golf, fishing, poker, and the Friday night out with the boys. Men rarely telephone one another to chat without an agenda. For men, friends usually come and go based upon activities rather than an enduring and trusting relationship.

Women tend to nurture a broad circle of close friends. The female style of participatory and interactive management in the workplace embodies a skill set well-suited for retirement. Women also tend to enjoy a broad range of common interests—a few photographs of children, grandchildren, or even the family pet are good starting points in the female bonding ritual. Moreover, women usually exercise a larger measure of control over a family social schedule that revolves around friends and activities.

In retirement, a supportive circle of close friends is invaluable. It is sustaining to have lasting friendships with members of the same sex with whom you can commiserate, confide, and share experiences. A large reservoir of contemporaries, who are circling and entering the retirement process, should make it relatively easy for men and women alike to build a post-retirement network of close friends. But for those inexperienced at actively seeking new friendships it may require a reassessment and planning process.

Finding Friends

1. First, make an extensive list of friends, relatives, coworkers, and social acquaintances with whom you regularly interact and feel comfortable. Add to the list friends from the past who have fallen through the cracks because of changing careers, geographic mobility, family breakups, and differing social circles. It may take weeks or even months to pull the list together—every day you may find that you add a new name or two. Once completed, evaluate and rank each person on the merits of a broadened relationship.

2. Make a second list, this one of activities that you truly enjoy. This list might seem quite simple to create, but all the enjoyments of a lifetime pose a wide variety of satisfying activities, and pursing one may cancel out the opportunity to pur-

sue another. Once the list is completed, weigh each option based on a scale of your personal satisfaction and fulfillment. It is important to be certain that the activity is sustainable and fits with the other realities and relationships in your life.

3. Match the lists to identify those special individuals with shared interests who fit with your definition of a potential lasting friend.

4. After deciding who might work best for you as a lasting friend, design a process to connect, and lay the foundations for a broadened friendship with them. Initial steps might include a simple phone call to share recent events and get caught up. You might invite them for lunch or to a social gathering. And the golf course, tennis courts, and card table are always good venues to renew friendships.

Depending upon your interests you might also join a travel, garden, investment, service, or hobby club to meet new people. Volunteer and church work can be used in a similar fashion.

Retirement is a marvelous time to become a true people person. One of the foremost positive predictors of a satisfying shift into the retirement mode is having a large, rich network of friends.

2. Reorienting Self-Esteem

Most employed individuals receive a measure of recognition, praise, and personal affirmation in the workplace. And that self-esteem boost disappears with retirement.

Retirement brings increased time spent at home with your spouse and other family members. In most instances, your retirement does little to profoundly alter their range of activities and interests. As before, they look to you for love and support and, as before, you receive their love and support. This, however, may not compensate for the recognition, power, and status you received at work.

In many instances your extended presence at home encroaches upon your spouse's territory, particularly if they retired before you and are used to having the house to themselves all day. Your spouse undoubtedly has an agenda and enjoys control over their daily activities. When you are home to stay, you receive recognition and accolades by fitting in with his or her plans—not necessarily by excelling at what you're doing.

You continue to shoulder your routine chores around the house, cutting the lawn, doing the dishes, paying the bills, and washing the cars. These tasks don't produce much acclaim, but they're usually increased when your partner realizes that you have more free time than they do. You may very well get new assignments such as tending the garden, picking up the dry cleaning, taking out the garbage, vacuuming the car, waiting for the repair man, walking the dog, and so on. Like it or not, the home crowd refuses to accept the previous power equation and pecking order that existed at work. The worst part of it is that you are now your own gopher and assistant.

But you must ask the question, "Why do I need so much recognition and stroking?" After all, you've proven your personal worth over a long career many times. Remind yourself that you're okay; you can justifiably live on your laurels and should not need a steady stream of recognition and praise. Thus, it is advisable to adopt a new way of thinking. Your self-esteem must be linked to your self-perception and feeling good about yourself instead of the motivators you had within the work environment.

Your self-esteem must be linked to your self-perception and feeling good about yourself instead of the motivators you had within the work environment.

Craft an approach to sustainable happiness through quiet, internal personal development. Place your focus on self-awareness, pleasing yourself, and heightened appreciation of idle simplicity. Self-esteem can be satisfied by inner fulfillment. As a respite from our busy lives, it is useful for most of us to just stop, think about the bigger picture, meditate about our place in the universe, and get new bearings.

In retirement we need to find meaning using a new mantra, one that emanates from inside. In Chapter 5 (on psychology), we delve more deeply into this issue.

3. It's a Beautiful Day in the Neighborhood

It may seem trite, but Mr. Rogers's introductory lines are right on target. Mixing the wonders of nature and the acuity of our senses makes our planet a magnificent place to live. A busy, cluttered life filled with the pressures of responsibility often dulls our natural ability to appreciate the physical world around us. What can be more exhilarating and calming than a leisurely hike through the woods on a warm, sunny day, or a bicycle ride with your children or grandchildren through the tree-lined streets and carefully manicured lawns in the neighborhood? Exiting the rat race frees up time to quietly contemplate and savor our surroundings. View life through the lens of nonjudgmental freedom, and much like the existentialist, decide for yourself what is true and beautiful, and ponder your place in the universe.

4. Spirituality and Gratitude

When former president Ronald Reagan was buried at the Ronald Reagan Presidential Library, the religious hymns, heartfelt eulogies, and prayers bidding him good-bye and wishing him a smooth journey into his next life were awe-inspiring. Sad events like this stir the passions of spirituality and create a mixture of grateful melancholy and joyful inspiration. Patriotic songs and love of country can evoke similar feelings. Most Americans feel grateful for the freedom and privilege they enjoy just by being citizens of this great country.

When you critically scrutinize it, you'll find that life is replete with acts of unexpected generosity, reverence, heroism, and caring. Taken altogether, this is a form of spirituality at its best. Spirituality enables you to appreciate life and live each day to its fullest. Give thanks each night for the good things that happened that day. Refocus on the spiritual aspects of living, and strive to be an apostle for goodness and empathy.

5. Focus on a Healthy Lifestyle

The process of aging is universal, though many of us are lucky enough to feel younger than our age and identify with a younger set. But you should not take risks trying to do things that stretched your capabilities twenty years ago. The black diamond ski slopes, bungee jumping, high-level whitewater rafting, and deep-sea scuba diving should generally be left to younger generations.

The black diamond ski slopes, bungee jumping, high-level whitewater rafting, and deep-sea scuba diving should generally be left to younger generations.

Retirement usually occurs close to the time when your biological and physiological reserves become non-renewable. For this reason you must conserve them with greater diligence than earlier in life. Regular trips to the physician for health promotion and disease prevention make good sense. Other recommendations include:

- Become your own medical advocate. Research your medical conditions. Insist that your physician provide you with reliable resources that guarantee informed decision-making. Select an accessible doctor who provides a conduit of information exchange. Your body belongs to you. It is your most valuable possession, and you are its primary caretaker and can best provide for its needs.

- Control addictions such as smoking and alcohol that may be exacerbated by increased free time and peer behavior in retirement communities.

- Follow a regular exercise program initiated with the advice and assistance of a professional trainer. This improves sleep habits and lessens the chances of developing diabetes, osteoporosis, hypertension, and obesity. Exercise releases body endorphins that produce a feeling of well-being, and it lessens body tension.

- Obesity has surpassed smoking as a health risk and is linked to a greater number of deaths per year than smoking. In roughly the last two decades, the percentages of people age sixty-five to seventy-four who are overweight or obese has risen from 57 to 73 percent. Controlled animal studies reveal that maintaining an ideal weight and ingesting fewer calories per day increases life expectancy. A strong case can be made for being thin—there are very few obese people who reach their ninetieth birthday. Maintain a balanced diet and a regular schedule of meals. Keep abreast of new dietary regimens that have proven safe and effective in losing weight and keeping it off. All programs designed to lose weight are most successful when combined with regular exercise.

- It is wise to seek medical advice if you are overweight. The intensive study of obesity is revealing a variety of underlying causes that are treatable. Moreover, there are many promising drugs in the pharmaceutical pipeline for weight control.

- Consider relaxation techniques such as meditation, yoga, self-hypnosis, breathing exercises, martial arts, prayer, massage, and communing with nature. These relaxation techniques help maintain a healthy body by connecting mind and body.

- The human body needs many essential vitamins and minerals. Most physicians advocate taking a multivitamin/multimineral supplement daily. These large pills are usually formulated to contain thirty or more ingredients that adequately cover basic daily requirements.

- Depression warrants special concern during retirement, since its incidence increases with age. In the elderly, depression often goes unrecognized and is often attributed erroneously to dementia. Common symptoms and complaints that may indicate depression include lingering sadness, decreased interest in normally pleasurable activities, weight loss, feelings of worthlessness or guilt, and recurrent thoughts of death. Suspecting and making the diagnosis is important since professionals, armed with potent antidepressant medications, can effectively treat this disorder. A rule of thumb is that if depression is prolonged beyond two weeks or is attended by suicidal thoughts, medical advice should be sought.

The human body is quite durable and even forgiving. One should not get too consumed with personal health. A common-sense approach to health that focuses on wellness, prevention, and healthy lifestyle pays huge dividends. You should also look to maintain and build your emotional and spiritual health. Consider the following to keep your mind as healthy as your body.

Reawaken the Extended Family

Busy schedules and geographic mobility often tear apart the extended family—aunts, uncles, cousins, nieces, nephews, in-laws. Unfortunately, in many families, relatives are seen only at weddings and funerals.

Family relationships are special, and the old expression "blood is thicker than water" is a valid truism.

But family relationships are special, and the old expression "blood is thicker than water" is a valid truism. Usually we have fond memories from childhood of our relatives and holidays, or reunions spent with one or the other side of the family. If an effort is made to renew the relationships, the warm recollections quickly foster the development of a new, meaningful kinship. And retirement is an ideal time to create new bonds within the family constellation.

Consider New Interests

Many people who enter retirement feel they will have too little to do to occupy their time. But often after six months, they complain they have insufficient time to get everything done and don't know how they had enough time to work prior to retirement.

The period leading up to retirement is a good time to start scouting out new activities to supplement your existing interests and time commitments. Look for enjoyable activities with obligations that match the amount of effort you wish to put forth. Many stimulating pursuits are low maintenance and offer flexible hours that fit into the rest of your schedule. Opportunities abound. You might wish to look at volunteer work in hospitals or museums, mentoring programs in elementary schools, or consulting work in a small business. And it's never too early to become one of those "thousand points of light" that meets unmet social needs. Frequently these forays into unfamiliar territory blossom into full-blown interests.

An outside meeting or small event each day is a good prescription to keep you connected and looking outward. Waking up with a blank schedule for two days is delightful, but for long periods it is vexing. Keep engaged with things you love and that which brings you happiness.

Case Study: Realignment in Retirement

Broad strategies to keep occupied and provide meaning in retirement vary widely. Below we hear from three retirees with vastly different ways of finding new passions to keep busy.

John, a productive and talented radiologist, voluntarily retired at age sixty. He abruptly severed all ties with his profession by surrendering his medical license and letting go of his medical circle of friends. His hobbies before retirement were model railroading and gardening. After retirement he became fully engaged in these two hobbies, working indoors during the winter on his model trains and outdoors during the summer on gardening. He has a magnificent flower garden that has been featured on garden television and in the gardening section of the newspaper. His train collection and fabulous track layout is mesmerizing to adults and children alike. He, like many others with hobbies that are important to them, cultivated a new identity based upon renewed passion for old interests.

Joan eased into retirement by refusing to schedule new psychiatric patients. But she retains her interest in medicine and devotes one afternoon a week to training residents at the local VA hospital. She continues to attend scientific meetings to keep her license current. Little has changed with her close circle of friends and social commitments. The real changes in retirement include an additional round of golf with her husband per week, spending more time fixing up the house, an additional week or two of travel per year, and many more sleepovers with her three young grandchildren. Her identity and enjoyments have changed little in retirement.

Jim, an engineer, is probably more typical of the mainstream retiree. Aside from working with a financial planner to evaluate the adequacy of his assets to support a sustainable retirement lifestyle, he planned little for his new life. The inactivity and mild depression that set in during the first three months of retirement convinced him that he needed more to keep his mind active. This prompted him to return to his previous job part-time. After a year he moved on to help his nephew establish a home rehab firm. He took art classes at night and found that painting fired his creativity and filled his schedule. Looking back, he concluded that it had taken over four years to settle into a new mission.

Personally Design Your Own Retirement

Retirement is entry into uncharted waters. Most people tend to base their expectations on the behaviors of others, and they often search for insights from anyone who has passed the threshold of retirement and is willing to talk about it. How often have you heard something similar to, "I don't want to retire like Uncle Joe, who didn't know what to do to keep occupied and died within six months of retirement"? Or, "I want to be just like Aunt Sarah, who loved to take her grandchildren on trips"? Often our expectations are prejudiced long before we think through the real issues of retirement.

But your retirement is just that: *Your* retirement. It is your experience and your life, and it has little or nothing to do with the experience and lives of those who have retired before you. Consequently, you do not need to dwell too long on the advice and retirement biographies of others, but rather, study yourself. You must know and please yourself. You have a unique set of gifts and interests upon which you should focus when planning retirement. This is the time to seize the day and make your special plans for you, to your specifications.

You do not need to dwell too long on the advice and retirement biographies of others, but rather, study yourself.

Diversification of Interests

In retirement it is important to select multiple activities that challenge both your mental and physical skills. This diversification is worthwhile should either your physical or mental capabilities deteriorate. For example, if you love tennis and have played for many years, what if you develop a rotator cuff or arthritic knee problem that severely restricts mobility? What can be substituted? It is a common observation that aging men and women switch from tennis to golf, and then from golf to less strenuous forms of exercise. Joggers who crowd sidewalks and hiking paths graduate to brisk walks and then leisurely nature walks.

In general, intellectual capabilities and mental faculties resist the insults of aging more than physical abilities. Activities such as bridge, chess, poker, puzzle making, birdwatching, reading, photography, collecting, patronizing the arts, and so on, are options that stimulate cerebrally and whose enjoyment is more apt to linger far into old age. The broader the range of your interests, the more new avenues exist to make equally satisfying substitutions.

Travel and Bridges to Retirement

Retirees often use travel, extended vacations, or sabbaticals to make the transition from work to leisure and symbolically leave the old self behind. Distant destinations muffle the distracting noise of past routines and permit unhurried reflection. Separation provides new perspectives about genuine interests and what new schedule you wish to implement to fill your valuable time.

Distant destinations muffle the distracting noise of past routines and permit unhurried reflection.

Travel opportunities abound that can both fulfill wanderlust and enrich your home life: Missionary work, college enrollment, mastering a foreign language, developing a flower and vegetable garden, cultural studies attached to an anthropological dig, hiking part of the Appalachian Trail, traveling coast-to-coast to visit the national parks in an RV, adding foreign elements to your collections, and many more. These new activities equate to a "time out" from life's routine for regrouping and setting the stage for a new identity. Although very different in context, they are akin to feelings you may have had early in life when you were overworked and felt burned out and wanted to just stop everything. Retirement allows this to happen.

A Scrapbook of Resources

Leading up to retirement, it is worthwhile to save articles and references that you come across in your reading and find especially meaningful to the process of retiring. The Internet is loaded with sites for retirees. A Google search for "retirement sites" resulted in a mind-numbing 850,000 hits. These form a veritable encyclopedia of information at your fingertips. You should also check out the library and acquaint yourself with its scope of reference texts, and take advantage of the calming environment of the local bookstore, where you can peruse recent publications. When you start to plan for retirement, having ready references at your fingertips helps with the process.

A BLUEPRINT FOR YOUR NEW MISSION

The aforementioned activities are focused on proactive planning and preparing the infrastructure on which to build your retirement. Unlike your employment, these activities have no links to power, influence, prestige, wealth, and social position. But they offer powerful survival skills and training strategies that solidly position a comfortable transition into retirement—making them just as important as your job skills. In the next chapter, you'll use these preparatory behaviors to help craft your new personal mission statement.

CHAPTER 2

Writing Your Personal Mission Statement

*W*hen you think of mission statements, you likely think of the way businesses define their goals and objectives, and how they promise to serve their customers. In more recent years, ambitious young people have used personal mission statements to think through career plans and set goals for the future. Many business schools have a leadership-course requirement for students to draft a personal mission statement.

With a lifetime of experience to draw from, a mission statement can be the unifier that brings together your identity, your life's purpose, your vision for the future, and the core values by which you plan to live the second half of your life.

But the creation of a personal mission statement can also be a starting point for seniors to begin the planning process for retirement. With a lifetime of experience to draw from, a mission statement can be the unifier that brings together your identity, your life's purpose, your vision for the future, and the core values by which you plan to live the second half of your life. In essence, it can be a blueprint that maps the path into this tricky life transition—a tool that creates a strategic framework for retirement that matches your special talents with your special interests.

THE CORPORATE BOARDROOM APPROACH

In the business world, companies large and small place great importance on developing a mission statement to define the domain and purpose of their activities. Usually senior executives of the company consider it an essential tool for organizational planning and corporate strategy, and they meticulously hammer out the document during off-site retreats and long hours of debate. Ideally, a mission statement, once crafted, is embedded throughout the corporate culture at all levels. And after being posted, widely communicated, and affixed to all company documents, it is pointed to as the business code of conduct and purpose.

In the corporate world, a mission statement is often broken into these four components:

1. The primary mission statement that embodies the purpose, goals, and objectives of the firm.

2. The vision statement that paints a picture of the future and states a goal for the company's situation in three to five years. This might be stated in terms of market share, revenue, profits, market dominance, mergers, or acquisitions.

3. A value statement that puts forth the high principles, morals, and spirituality that underpin the firm's behavior. Common to these statements are terms such as "respect," "teamwork,"

"community citizenship," "environmental sensitivity," and "customer service."

4. An identity statement that communicates to all stakeholders where the firm fits in society. In many religious organizations and subsidiaries of larger companies, the identity is linked to the parent organization.

There is a typical lingo for corporate mission statements that paints an idealized view of the firm and manufactures a collective purpose for all employees. Terms such as "superior quality," "service to the customer," "major player," "sustainable growth," "visionary leadership," and "exemplary corporate citizen" are commonplace. But just the upper echelon of the business pyramid creates business mission statements. And in many companies the views of this small group of senior executives do not dovetail with those of middle management and the frontline workers. Consequently, the mission statement often does not trickle down and populate throughout the entire organization. As Steven Covey in his book *First Things First* observes, in the majority of businesses there is often little buy-in to company mission statements at the lower levels. This is in stark contrast to a personal mission statement—you get to compose something that applies only to you and with which you agree 100 percent.

A Typical Corporate Statement

Here is the Mission and Purpose statement from Pfizer, a large pharmaceutical company:

> *We will become the world's most valued company to patients, customers, colleagues, investors, business partners, and the communities where we work and live. We dedicate ourselves to humanity's quest for longer, healthier, happier lives through innovation in pharmaceutical, consumer, and animal health products.*
>
> The statement certainly contains colossal goals and high purpose, but to an average employee it might seem somewhat esoteric and disconnected from their daily experience on the job. It has no unique personal meaning.

YOUR PERSONAL MISSION STATEMENT

Although quite similar in structure to corporate mission statements, personal mission statements are quite different in context and feel. They are warm and fuzzy and have a direct connection to who you are. They are colored by your own special aspirations and values. Just like corporate mission statements, personal mission statements are often superlative and highly benevolent in their content. But if honestly crafted, a clear picture usually emerges that brings together all the variables and personal objectives that are a part of the passage into retirement. Personal mission statements can put both your objective and subjective considerations under the magnifying glass.

To some, crafting a personal mission statement at this late date seems ridiculous. After all, the majority of retirees have some sense of mission and an outline for retirement without having to write it down. But a retirement plan could lack thoroughness and clarity if you relied entirely on memory and the impulses of the moment. Even if you have terrific, insightful, and dazzling ideas one day, it is unlikely you will remember all of them if you don't write them down. And complete active recall of our personal insights does not improve with age. Moreover, fleeting thoughts and ideas that randomly stir within our conscious thought are not usually indicative of what we want and need in the big picture.

When you write down your mission statement, you always have the option to enhance, amend, reformulate, and update the plan.

Writing down a personal mission statement helps you focus on the big picture. When you write it down, you always have the option to enhance, amend, reformulate, and update the plan. It also gives the contents time to ferment and mature.

A written document also affords you the option and time to collaborate with friends and run your thoughts by your significant other and other family members. This intimate focus group is a useful sounding board and can give great and important feedback. In addition, the success of your mission statement often rests with the buy-in and support you receive from your family circle.

Why You Need a Mission Statement

Some of you might still question the utility of a retirement mission statement or even consider it a waste of time. But unlike other phases in life, retirement is not tightly choreographed with goals and objectives from outside sources. No outlines exist to indicate what retirement is for. Retirement does not come with directions. There is no social standard for retirement. Exemplary retirees are infrequently featured in the print media as role models. Most friends and family are reluctant to offer concrete advice, because it might prove harmful and cause blame. Consequently, retirement can be shrouded with ambiguity. This churning of uncertainty magnifies the assault on self and self-esteem brought about by the transition from employment or underemployment. Probably at no other time in life is one in greater need of reflective guidance and diligent planning of tailoring goals and ideals to guide many years.

Retirement does not come with directions.

On the positive side, retirement brings the gift of time, plus the chance to make choices for yourself on how you'll spend your time. In this new framework, satisfaction increasingly comes from within and success from self-starting. You do not have someone else or your job telling you what to do. You have the latitude to unleash your creativity and personal expression to achieve a new model for living. A personal mission statement can help provide the keys to open the doors to the paths you wish to follow.

Questions to Consider

When you begin crafting your mission statement, pose a series of questions to yourself. This can help frame the issues and add the necessary ingredients to your statement. Here are a few random questions to get you started:

- What new directions would I like to pursue?

- Do I want to work part-time or do consulting work?

- What do I want to leave to my heirs and charity?

- What means do I have to give back to my community?

- How active do I wish to be in the church, mosque, or synagogue?

- How can I share my experience through mentoring?

- Is my mission statement going to be compatible with the other realities in my life?

- What new and old friendships do I wish to nurture in retirement?

- What new social and athletic activities might I like?

- How will my family relationships change?

- How do I stay healthy and active?

- Would I like to move to a retirement community or warmer climate?

- How do I plan to handle my finances?

- What can I do to create a bridge between work and retirement?

GETTING STARTED

A personal mission statement should act as a compass to guide the transition into retirement. For some the task will seem easy, while others may find it very difficult. Either way, you must first resolve to devote time to just writing down your general ideas. Try to objectively review your true feelings and inner needs. Appraise how things are now and how they could be improved in the future. Allow time to let your reasoning blossom and original thoughts crystallize into well-formed ideas. Brainstorm to add new possibilities. Rank the important items, rate the chances for positive change, and weave a new, ideal plan for your retirement. Analyze all your answers, and focus your ideas. A mission statement that is a true reflection of your being takes time to evolve—time that you actually have to set aside just for this task.

True feelings and honest objectivity often make a personal mission statement a deeply intimate document that you want to keep confidential. If you are uncomfortable sharing the contents with friends and family, disclose only what you think is safe and appropriate. Writing this statement is a very private undertaking; you get to decide how much of it and what parts other people see.

Writing It All Down

Your written mission can be as simple or complex as you wish to make it. Once you get started, especially if you provide adequate time for thoughts to germinate, it usually evolves into a lengthy document that addresses all the options and variables that confront you. If you permit the process to take root, you may find that even six to eight pages of written text are inadequate to corral your thoughts and feelings. Write as much as you feel is necessary, and then reevaluate, edit, and rank the ideas according to importance.

The mission must reconcile your aspirations with physical capabilities. Most would consider a full marathon, a bicycle ride across America, or a climb to the summit of Mt. McKinley outside the realm of possibility. Remember, your physical endurance and resilience is on the downward slope of the curve. Although you may have plenty of time, trying to recapture your earlier ability in contact athletics and highly competitive sports will likely be frustrating unless you spar only with individuals within your age bracket. Moreover, family and friends will usually act as a reality check and hasten to point out the folly of an impossible dream.

Existing relationships and previous commitments must be factored into your mission statement. Family needs and financial resources have to be considered. And the mission plan should be flexible enough to adjust to the "what if" scenarios that so often shroud the passage into retirement. It is no secret that the unforeseen and improbable can derail even the best-laid plans.

No standardized process or optimal method exists to instruct the individual crafting a mission statement. It is not an exam but rather a creative voyage of discovery. The final result is like a roadmap for the future.

Five Issues Pivotal to Most Personal Mission Statements

1. Generous Behaviors

Throughout life we add to a reservoir of intellectual, social, and economic capital. To have been blessed to live in our open society where freedom provides the opportunity to enjoy a wealth of opportunities makes people grateful, and retirement is a wonderful time in life to show appreciation by being generous in giving back and helping others. There is an urgent need for role models, mentors, and coaches at all levels of society (more on this in Chapter 24). Everyone has some special gift to give and share that can be a worthy part of a mission statement or even a centerpiece of it.

2. Renewing Family Life

Family takes on greater importance when you're home to stay. Retirement is a time to foster better family ties. It is a time to resolve any lingering undercurrents that relate to long-ago arguments or disappointments that are now irrelevant. It is a time to build on the love family members share for one another, and to reach out to your children and grandchildren and other members of the extended family. Financial assistance, sharing, reunions at vacation homes or destinations, nurturing and caring for grandchildren, a new family project or shared hobby, encouragement for a son's or daughter's career change or new directions, and other such activities can enhance family life and unity. We all know it is difficult to change established family paradigms. But retirement is a great time to focus on family harmony and rejuvenate commonalties and warm feelings. Any mission statement that does not feed on close relationships within family is lacking.

3. Personal Interests

Many of us are reluctant to retire because we tend to think we don't have the hobbies or interests necessary to occupy our time. However, you don't need well-developed hobbies to pursue new interests of your choice. How often has each of us said, "I would like to do such and such, if only I had the time"? Well, now you have the time. You can take that trip to Antarctica, build a workshop in your basement, and take the grandchildren to a national park. Rekindle old interests, learn new skills, expand your horizons, and take risks. Search out a group with whom to share these interests. As Rosalyn Russell says in *Auntie Mame,* "Life's a banquet, but most poor bastards are starving to death." Inject your intent to sample a wider variety from the banquet table of life into your mission statement.

4. Health

Health is always a number one priority. Poor health can preempt any exciting plans for retirement. If medical concerns and expenses consume your activities, it leaves little time or money for enjoyment. No one is immune to the medical problems that multiply and compound with aging. But we can try to prevent the misfortune of disease by paying greater attention to the disciplined behaviors that support your best possible health. A mission statement should contain a commitment to a healthy lifestyle. You owe it to yourself.

5. Finances

Having enough money does not guarantee either happiness or a purposeful life. However, it does provide options and flexibility. Add a financial strategy, and plan to your mission statement to keep the doors open to fulfill the rest of your mission.

A Personal Mission Statement

Below is an outline of a typical personal mission statement, divided into the components of the business model: Mission, Vision, Values, and Identity Statements.

Mission

- Provide unconditional love to our grandchildren. Help my daughter with a problem child who is strung out on drugs. Take steps to ensure that resources are available for any grandchild who wishes to go to college.

- Share my expertise in art history and accounting with my contemporaries by giving courses to retirees and lectures to service clubs on related topics.

- Polish my skills at golf and fly-fishing, and increase my circle of friends with similar interests.

- Start to divest my collections of antique toys and baseball trading cards using the Internet.

- Become more active in the church, and develop counseling services for troubled youngsters.

Vision

- Become settled into our retirement home in Arizona, and cultivate a new circle of close friends there.

- Give my best effort toward making the small novelty shop we purchased profitable within three years.

- Optimize my lifestyle in order to try for twenty more years of life.

Values

- Allow caring and giving to guide my actions, and not jealousy, intolerance, or prejudice.
- Live by religious values, and place a greater emphasis on my spiritual life.
- Focus on a healthy lifestyle, and give up cigar smoking.

Identity

- Accept the fact that I am retired: Mellow out, relax, and enjoy the privilege.
- Adjust to a new role as caregiver, nurturer of the family, and homemaker.
- Feel proud and authentic for having finished one successful career, and be confident of self-worth in any new venture.

PUTTING THE MISSION STATEMENT TO WORK

A mission statement is an excellent planning tool to organize your goals and purpose in advance of retirement. You'll need to do some significant critical thinking and soul-searching to capture the radiant possibilities that lie beyond the threshold of retirement. A well-tailored mission statement takes time to evolve, perhaps even months or a few years. Once you start in earnest, you will find that each day brings new ideas to the surface, and with time your thoughts take shape. The final product gives you a reliable set of signposts that point the way into retirement.

If you live your mission statement, it is like writing the final chapter in your own autobiography.

After you finish writing a mission statement, it needs to be implemented. With that thought in mind, it is worthwhile to review it daily to keep it fresh. Some people like to hang their mission statement in a conspicuous place and measure the accomplishments of each day against specific goals and objectives. Over time, you develop a keen awareness of your progress. If you live your mission statement, it is like writing the final chapter in your own autobiography.

CHAPTER 3

Building on Past Pleasures

*H*appiness is subjective and often difficult to quantify, but it's inarguable that retirees are entitled to their fair share of happiness. Each individual interprets what defines a fair share differently—expectations and perceptions are everything when describing what happiness is. Or as an often-recited phrase from Shakespeare states: "There is nothing either good or bad, but thinking makes it so." To carry it another step further, it is said that one man's trash is another man's treasure.

In most of us, those bygone golden days of innocence and simplicity still live on in our hearts and minds.

When we reflect upon the pleasures of life, most reside in our memories and are often far removed from the realities of the present. Each of us can recall many unique experiences when happiness seemed real and life was good. In those times, joy and excitement were tangible and did not need to be examined or defined. Now you have the time to revisit those special times and explore those that can be reincarnated as a part of your retirement experience.

There are few among us who don't think that the good old days were all that good, and while everyone is entitled to their opinion, older generations definitely come from a much simpler and more innocent era. Our music had melodies with lyrics that made sense. Our card and board games were interactive happenings and very different from to-day's hours of TV and computer games. Kids had one-speed bicycles to leisurely cruise the neighborhood without a sporting event, dance class, or violin lesson on each day's schedule. Kids learned sports through doing them and not through endless clinics, private lessons, expert supervision, and interclub matches. Simple picnics with box lunches were a big treat, as opposed to a sweaty day at a mega-theme park riding the rides. Tickets in the bleachers at the baseball park cost fifty cents. Teenagers had formal dates with curfews rather than just mingling in a crowd. The pace was slower, competition was less pervasive, and the noise of daily life was less intrusive. Moreover, college was affordable, and a college education was of less importance. There was a greater sense of honesty, integrity, and spirituality—rather than legislation—that controlled human behavior. Concern for your neighbor was deeply rooted, and religion was more central to daily life.

In most of us, those bygone golden days of innocence and simplicity still live on in our hearts and minds. They are imprinted within our very beings and form the basis of our definition of happiness. Retirement is a time when we can reexamine these satisfying moments earlier in our lives.

OUTSIDE PRESSURES

Society subtly encourages retirees to prove to others that they're comfortable with retirement. To concede otherwise is to admit to a failure of some sort. If you are grumpy or whiny, you receive little sympathy—you're retired! What could possibly be wrong? The general belief is that retirement is cushy and heavenly. If you complain, you may be viewed as ungrateful or as having unrealistic expectations. Consequently, few recent retirees feel completely at ease with expressing and elaborating upon the natural difficulties that plague all retirements.

This need to seem constantly happy and fulfilled often stimulates a not-so-subtle competition between retirees. Without the prestige of gainful employment, the number of trips taken and countries visited becomes more important. Bragging rights also link to the location and size of holiday homes, number of grandchildren, social galas, and golf handicaps. Many accoutrements of affluence are used to cover any indication that things may not be going well. Indeed, in the American culture, whenever genuine purpose or meaning is under attack or has been eroded, the default or substituted meaning and purpose almost always become wealth and money.

But wealth does not equate to happiness. Happiness is an internal state, one that is dependent upon a lifetime of personal experience.

In the American culture, whenever genuine purpose or meaning is under attack or has been eroded, the default or substituted meaning and purpose almost always become wealth and money.

Unwanted Intruders

Our desire to capture past pleasures must be balanced with medical realities. The normal aging process can erode vitality and limit our alternatives. Advancing age may increase our need to depend upon others to meet basic needs. We may be confronted with a serious illness or unexpected hospital stay. This in turn may require ratcheting down our independent living and require a move into a grown child's house, assisted living, or even a nursing home.

Also, less severe medical conditions can become interlopers to our plans. To cite the most common, old orthopedic injuries and degenerative arthritis afflict the vast majority of seniors. For these individuals, just rising in the morning is an exercise in new anatomical points of pain, stiffness, and soreness that the old sites are causing. And strenuous physical activities usually cause the new sites to multiply and the old sites to exacerbate. Unfortunately, aspirin, Tylenol, nonsteroidal anti-inflammatory drugs (NSAIDs), and COX-2 inhibitor medications provide only temporary relief and do not reverse the underlying disorder. Moreover, these medications can produce serious side effects, such as life-threatening gastrointestinal bleeding. All medication must be viewed from the perspective of risk versus benefit and under the observation of a doctor.

It is obvious that we are all at risk for medical afflictions that compel changes in lifestyle and undermine even the best-laid plans. Life is unpredictable, and no one can divine where the lightning might strike. You should pursue only activities that both satisfy and fulfill you while not putting you in any physical danger.

REPLAYING HAPPY TIMES

Looking back over our lives, all of us can recall especially fond memories and moments of happiness. Review this cherished collection, and focus on the ones with relevance to present circumstances. Can the jubilation, curiosity, liberation, and passion you once felt be unlocked and brought forward into the present and future?

Yes—but realistically. Early interests may exceed existing resources. A steady diet of thirty-six holes of golf, open tennis tournaments, and jogging five miles a day are usually activities of the past. If your passion was the opera and live stage productions, you are limited if you've moved to a smaller retirement community away from the big city. A steady diet of travel to your previous destinations may deplete your pocketbook and be too physically tiring. Important collections may need to be converted to cash rather than added to. Nevertheless, for most people there are many exhilarating interests residing in the past that may be simple and doable and are just waiting to be given a new life.

Every new choice you make has an opportunity cost. In colloquial terms, "opportunity cost" means, "You can't have your cake and eat it too." Any major changes in retirement can reassign limited resources. For example, a permanent move to a southern retirement community, a steady diet of travel, or the purchase of an expensive, dream vacation home are types of decisions that eliminate many other opportunities. How do you connect with your grandchildren at home when you live halfway across the country or are always out of town? How do you retain your social relationships and remain active in any clubs you belong to? Weigh all of your options, because everything has a trade-off. Consider all the people your decision will affect, and pursue those activities that offer the most utility. Leave as many doors open as possible.

Moreover, retirement pursuits must maintain self-worth and integrity. This may seem obvious, but occasionally unbridled leisure seems to act as an invitation to just let things slide. Without a schedule and with little responsibility, some may indulge in excesses such as "social" drinking throughout the day, obsessive betting on the ponies or online gambling, and other addictions that preempt a normal, healthy routine. Follow-up appointments to see the doctor may be ignored, family celebrations allowed to slip by unnoticed, and annual trips to visit friends and relatives postponed. The home and personal appearance can be neglected and the social orbit downsized. It is clear that in retirement you need as much discipline and take-charge behavior as you had while you were working to avoid these downward spirals.

Leave as many doors open as possible.

Retirement is a milestone where society condones and even invites the individual to break the previous frame of routine. Why not seize the opportunity to exploit this permissive latitude to pursue your core interests? Do some soul searching. Evaluate what has given you pleasure and fire in the past that can mesh with your current life circumstances. Add change and acceptable risks with new activities that offer challenges and surprises. Create a new framework for your life.

Activity Evaluation

Objectively review the activities you have chosen for retirement to ensure they're achievable. Are resources available? What are the odds they will meet your expectations? Does your family support them? To answer these questions, place the activity under the magnifying glass of the five Ps:

- **Passion:** Does it leverage your genuine interests from the past and present?

- **Place:** Do the circumstances surrounding your life support the activity?

- **People:** Will the new and old circles of relationships mesh with your revised menu of activities?

- **Posterity:** Does the activity produce a legacy that benefits the community and reflects favorably on the way you wish to be remembered?

- **Perspective:** Are the goals you set anchored in reality and not just pipe dreams?

LETTING GO

The cynics and whiners say that life is unfair, the road to hell is paved with good intentions, and only "cream and bastards" rise to the top. Certainly as we age, the idealism and pure inspiration of youth are bent out of shape by small betrayals, disappointments, and the insults of daily living. However, what does this really matter in the grand scheme of things? Why ruminate on things from the past that can be left in the past and no longer remain a threat or a part of reality? A negative countenance and chronic complaining have always been and will always be the pathway to isolation.

Human behavior is strongly conditioned from early experience, and as we grow up and mature, it becomes remarkably repetitive. Psychological principles teach that early emotional conflicts may produce consistent neurotic behavior that is difficult to break, and is in fact so ingrained that it severely impairs the decision-making process. This often produces repetitive cycles of self-defeating behaviors that are barriers to happiness. Indeed, mental health counselors devote the majority of their time trying to help patients break the repetitive cycles of unhealthy and self-destructive conduct.

A negative countenance and chronic complaining have always been and will always be the pathway to isolation.

Unfortunately, despite all attempts to resolve these negative emotional problems from the past, they sometimes spill over into adult life and become a part of the person's basic personality. Emotional disturbances always leave footprints that are not easily washed away by the elements of time. But, if possible, retirement is a time to try to let go of conflict and emotional static. If you have trouble doing this alone, seek professional counseling to assist in dealing with your demons. Learn to focus on renewal of those things connected with delight, adventure, and excitement, and let go of those things that caused you pain in the past that has lingered.

TAKE-HOME LESSONS FROM THE WORKPLACE

Reviewing your work experience can produce a balance sheet of likes and dislikes and provide great ideas for retirement. What activities have fueled your best performance and given you a sense of accomplishment? If you can identify the outstanding attributes of the work experience, you might consider incorporating some of these into your retirement planning.

Create a list of both the best and worst features of your job. Rate the importance of each positive and negative feature on a scale of one to three—very important, somewhat important, and not important. Once your list and evaluation are complete, focus on those items that you rated as very important and that clearly create job satisfaction and fulfillment. Finally, write out a design for the workplace that creates the optimal model for meeting the needs and wants of the employee. This prototype then becomes a blueprint against which you can evaluate future activities.

When looking at this blueprint against your possible retirement activities, you might ask some of the following questions:

1. Do you prefer working alone or as part of a team or partnership?

2. Are there specific tasks at which you excel and that you find stimulating? Could these talents and passions form the basis for a part-time job, an entrepreneurial venture, or a volunteer project?

3. Of those friendships you made in the workplace, which ones can be carried over into retirement? How do you plan to do this?

4. What motivates your behavior? Is monetary compensation the primary driver, or is recognition of a job well done of equal importance? If you give to charity, do you wish to remain an anonymous donor?

5. How could you make home and your community a better place to "work"?

6. Does the company provide any benefits to retired workers? Could you be classified as "emeritus" and continue to be included in and attend company celebrations?

7. Reflect on your many years of work experience, and make a judgment on whether the workplace improved over the years. In talking with a variety of retirees from many sectors of the business world, it is apparent that stress levels and hassle factors have increased during the past thirty years due to rising competition, automation, and regulation. But on the flip side, some changes have dramatically improved the work environment and system. If you have seen positive changes, ask if those changes can help you manage your retirement.

8. What made your company a good place to work?

You can pose a long list of questions about your current or past work environments that sheds light on what you enjoy. Also reflect on the fact that employees, both men and women, often behave differently at work than at home. How often have you heard contrasting comments about behavior such as, "He's domineering at home but meek at the office," or, "She's warm and friendly at work but distant at home"? It is not unusual that a Dr. Jeckyll resides at home while a Mr. Hyde dwells in the workplace, or vice versa. Behaviors and agendas at home and away are often vastly different, and this dichotomy of roles and personalities needs to be reckoned with in the retirement, when there is generally only home.

The treadmill of employment often makes the balancing act between work and home difficult. Long hours and work-related travel limit daily interaction and sharing with your spouse and community. Many couples literally go their separate ways and live most of the daylight and evening hours in totally different worlds. Sometimes working couples are like strangers sharing the frame but not the picture and art of life. With retirement there is a need to appraise these separate paths and integrate them into a new frame with a new background. Discussing the new scenario should smooth the transition.

> *Sometimes working couples are like strangers sharing the frame but not the picture and art of life.*

Creatively conjecturing a retirement model based upon happiness from the employment years can be insightful and fun, and it will definitely positively influence your decisions. All of us are creatures of habit and reinforced behaviors. Select those that have served you well.

Case Studies: Leveraging the Past into the Present

Chad fondly remembers a happy childhood and family life. The freedom he enjoyed provided a platform for creativity and exploration. His mother fed his curiosity as they visited museums, read books, made puzzles, talked about Indians, and developed collections. Old, discarded devices like toasters, radios, and tools were his to break down and look inside. Chad's mother patiently took the time to answer any and all of his questions. Chad had great fondness for this freewheeling and stimulating time of life.

His thirst for knowledge was later quenched with his study of the biological sciences, and Chad became a physician. His medical practice imposed a regimented schedule and disciplined adherence to structured treatment protocols. After retirement at age sixty, he looked for outlets for creative expression. He took the equivalent of two semesters of business courses in the Entrepreneurial Center, after which he became a limited partner in a venture capital start-up fund that focused on health care. His background made him an expert on new-product evaluation and marketing. This part-time activity has contributed to his becoming a high-net-worth retiree, while at the same time satisfying the intellectual curiosity, creativity, and diversity of interests that were a product of his boyhood.

In his youth, Tad went to camp in northern Minnesota for eight summers. Activities at camp included sports, the study of Indian arts and culture, fishing, and canoe trips. His favorite were the seven- to ten-day canoe trips that required camping in tents in the northern wilderness. The shared hardships bonded the campers together as friends and as a team. The final three summers at camp, Tad was recruited to be a counselor and directed and led these canoe trips. This signature experience reinforced his self-confidence and love of the northern wilderness. He emerged as a leader with fine mentoring skills.

Tad became a successful insurance agent who semiretired at age fifty-nine by cutting back to service just a few accounts. To fill his time, he actively participates in two programs to assist and guide troubled teenagers. In addition, he coaches a T-ball and Junior League baseball team. The family retreat is an isolated cottage located in northern Maine on a scenic lake. In retirement, Tad has duplicated and drawn upon those happy days back when he was a youngster at camp in Minnesota.

Joe experienced hard times during the Depression. Money was scarce, and Joe's folks had to make many sacrifices just to get by. They had no funds to send any of the children to college. Joe went to work in a car transmission factory. For twenty-five years he was a loyal and conscientious production worker. But with the changes in the new economy, he was downsized out of a job, and a generous severance package was added to his 401(k) plan. This windfall amply supported his quest for further education. In addition, his life's savings have become sufficient to provide for the college education of his two children.

As a child, Joe loved books. A prized possession of his family was *The World Book Encyclopedia*, which he read from cover to cover. After becoming a factory worker, he had always dreamed of going back to school to get a degree and becoming a teacher.

He enrolled in a two-year computer-programming course. Upon graduation he accepted a twenty-hour-per-week job with an insurance company. His desire to be a teacher has been met by teaching computer classes. Twice a year, Joe conducts a course for seniors in a "learning-in-retirement" program, plus he volunteers in the public school system to teach second- and third-grade pupils.

These snapshots are typical of retirees who have looked back on their lives and focused on creating new interests based upon earlier dreams and gratifying experiences. It is a worthwhile exercise for those approaching retirement to identify hallmarks in their lives that have generated enthusiasm and passion. Retirement provides a unique opportunity to build around those themes.

CHAPTER 4

Life Inventories

*T*he early days of retirement are an excellent time to take inventory, tie up loose ends, and get your affairs in order. When you're busy balancing your career with your family life and obligations, it's easy to neglect timely reviews of wills, trusts, legacy giving, power of attorney, insurance, and so on. For this reason, getting everything in order as soon as possible after you retire is a good idea—it may have been years since you've thought about and revised these crucial decisions and documents.

No matter your age, it is never too early to answer certain critical questions. Who will manage your affairs in the event of disability or death? Who will know where your important documents are? Who handles your accounting, legal, and tax matters? How do you wish for the assets to be divided, and what special bequests are there?

Getting everything in order as soon as possible after you retire is a good idea— it may have been years since you've thought about and revised crucial decisions and documents.

Retirement highlights the need to take inventory. If you haven't done so already, or if you need to make changes, consider reviewing the following matters:

1. As startling as it may seem, most Americans do not have wills crafted by an attorney. Wills and other agreements must be made if you have specific intentions you want carried out. If you die without a will (intestate), the courts, in a lengthy process, decide who gets your assets based upon the laws of the state in which you live. As well as composing a will with an attorney, you should walk the executor you appoint for your estate through your estate plan and any special provisions, as well as make sure he or she knows where your will is. Also, only you know what might be best for your family; you may wish to discuss the basic provisions of the will with them once it is officially settled.

2. On the medical side, you may want to execute a living will to provide instructions to your family and physician in the event that you have a terminal condition that is irreversible, incurable, and untreatable, or you are in a permanent unconscious state. (As a safeguard, legally two doctors must concur if treatment is to be withheld.) A Do Not Resuscitate (DNR) order is a written medical order given by the physician that cardiopulmonary resuscitation (CPR) not be administered. A health care power of attorney can be executed to appoint an attorney-in-fact to make decisions about authorizing or refusing treatment for you if you are unable to do so for yourself. As of 2002, only 15 percent of Americans had completed these advanced directive documents. But they are extremely

useful in guiding medical decision making, and the forms are easily obtained and completed. Hospitals are mandated by Congress to inform patients about advanced directives and provide the standardized forms. Most physician and law offices also offer assistance.

3. Evaluate the need for long term care medical insurance: A year in a nursing home or assisted living facility may cost between $45,000 and $90,000. Less than one in five men and one in three women end up in a nursing facility, and the average stay is less than a year. Since insurance premiums are high and the contracts often contain exclusions and limits, you must carefully weigh the premium costs versus the potential benefits.

4. Review your long-term plans for charitable giving. Discuss the necessary trust instruments to carry out your plan with your lawyer and estate advisers.

5. Have your advisers review any trust agreements to ensure they comply with current federal tax law and maximize estate tax exemptions.

6. If you have a safety deposit box or secure hiding place for valuables, inventory the contents. Then consider consolidating your important documents and valuables into one location that is conveniently located to allow easy retrieval. Possibly, allow a trustworthy person, close relative, or estate executor access to your safety deposit box.

7. Make a written inventory of the contents of your home and personal possessions. Then, use a video camera to make an

insurance audit of your home. Write out specific instructions for distribution of collections, furniture, jewelry, and personal effects to your heirs.

8. Make a master list that catalogs the following items. Store the actual documents in a safety deposit box or a secure, fire-protected area separate from the location where you store this master list, where you should also keep copies of the documents.

Birth dates and birth certificates

Wills and trust agreements

Social Security numbers

Passports

Marriage license and civil certificates

Vehicle registrations and titles

Property deeds

Insurance policies

Health insurance and long-term care policies

Military discharges

Burial plots and funeral arrangements

Living wills and durable power of attorney

Warranties

Important agreements

Instructions for the executor of your estate

9. Craft a list of your advisers with contact information and a brief paragraph detailing what each has been placed in charge of.

   Lawyers

   Accountants

   Insurance agents

   Financial planner

   Brokers

10. Compile a list of your financial accounts, and include the account numbers and how they may be accessed.

    Bank accounts

    Brokerage accounts

    Online stock trading accounts

    Retirement accounts, including the addresses and phone numbers of administrators

11. Catalog all other important miscellaneous information.

    List of credit cards and numbers

    Frequent flyer numbers

    Club memberships

    Stock certificates, bonds, IOUs, written agreements

    Outstanding loans and obligations

12. Craft a master balance sheet to be annually updated that contains all assets and liabilities and produces a net-worth figure for your household.

Keeping your affairs organized brings many benefits to both your heirs and your retirement planning. It is expeditious to have a consolidated personal reference file, and this ease of access helps with getting your affairs in order.

Moreover, openly discussing your affairs with key beneficiaries and family often affords new insights into how you wish to craft your legacy. A thorough description of your personal paper trail and advisers will definitely make matters easier for your descendants. Moreover, sharing this knowledge with your children will position them to better serve your needs in retirement.

SECTION II:

Navigating the Emotional Transition

CHAPTER 5

A Psychological Perspective

*I*n a discussion group with retired managers from an aerospace company, the following question was raised: What features from your work experience do you miss most in retirement?

Two responded that they missed the steady stream of interaction with clients and coworkers and felt somewhat isolated. One complained of a loss of power because she no longer had subordinates to lead and had to be her own gopher and secretary. One found the freedom and necessity to create a new routine disturbing, since during the thirty years of employment he was constantly barraged with incoming demands that completely filled his daily schedule. One frankly stated that his fixed income left him with little discretionary income to permit impulse spending and a more extravagant lifestyle. One missed the intensity and challenges of the workplace, and proffered that the home routine provided an insufficient amount of intellectual stimulation and sense of competition. One felt a sense of being imprisoned at home, and mentioned that this shut down any fond thoughts of adventure and indiscretion. One individual, who had no serious complaint, did mention that he was gradually driving his wife crazy by overdosing her with togetherness. This broad range of perspectives on what was sacrificed with retirement is actually quite commonplace—retirement will bring different emotions for everyone.

The psychological adjustment to retirement is different for each individual. Even if you are the CEO or top dog, life's journey usually leaves behind some elusive dreams and unmet expectations. Those who do achieve "self-actualization," the worn expression used to measure the ultimate success in life, are probably the exception rather than the rule.

Even if you are the CEO or top dog, life's journey usually leaves behind some elusive dreams and unmet expectations.

Moreover, as we age, our personality becomes more defined and less amenable to change. The image of self and what psychologists call "ego assets" accumulate and solidify as the years pass. There are many other factors that will influence these emotions as well: ethnicity, gender, race, health status, educational achievement, wealth, and—heading the list—expectations. With these variances, it's easy to see why no two individuals share an identical emotional backdrop as they transition into retirement.

As you enter middle age, the attitude of invincibility and toughness that characterizes youth often fades and is replaced with a more realistic assessment of life and physical limitations. As a result, many older individuals tend to worry more and be more concerned with bodily functions and sensitive to the minor hazards of daily living. Seeing friends with serious illnesses produces a keen awareness of the medical problems that come with aging. Health articles and programs, as well as the deluge of pharmaceutical advertisements, list early symptoms of disease—symptoms that often duplicate the symptoms that all of us experience from time to time. As a result, we monitor the workings of our bodies more closely and take minor complaints more seriously. It is similar to freshman medical students who start to dwell on their minor somatic complaints after they note that many of them are associated with one or more of the horrendous diseases they are studying.

Normal aging has both an upside and a downside. On the one hand, your physical reserves diminish, and medical limitations can curb some pleasurable activities. On the other, experience brings seasoning and a fuller appreciation of life. Your maturity nurtures feelings of sentimental attachment and appreciation that distill into greater empathy and caring for others. The sadness of losing parents, siblings, and good friends produces a greater sensitivity to the seasons and cycle of life. Although these losses may be devastating, they still are an integral part of a rich emotional life.

Gender Differences

There is a lack of hard data comparing the differences in the severity of the retirement transition between sexes. Discussions with scores of men and women suggest that the transition into retirement is equally challenging for both. This parity seems to hold true especially for the higher-paying managerial and supervisory jobs where career advancement has played a major role in fulfillment and self-worth.

But the ego strengths and personality traits that are carried into retirement do seem to exhibit gender differences. Upbringing and competitive pressures influence men to center on rivalry and action rather than feeling. In comparison, women learn to be more nurturing and sociable. The female mold tends to fit better into retirement—women seem more prepared to leave behind the competitive atmosphere of the workplace than men.

AT FIRST GLANCE

Most people enter retirement exhilarated by the thought of no alarm clock or fixed schedule. You are rid of the boss, deadlines, paperwork, difficult coworkers, and troublesome customers. However, a few months into retirement, any negative feelings you may have had about your job and work often seem to fade into oblivion, replaced with an idealized nostalgia. Perhaps it's a case of "absence makes the heart grow fonder." These feelings can be very persuasive and unsettling, but there is an easy remedy for this irrational sentimentality.

A few months into retirement, any negative feelings you may have had about your job and work often seem to fade into oblivion, replaced with an idealized nostalgia.

First, reenact your former work habits by setting the alarm clock to 7:00 a.m., getting up and putting on a work suit, and then fighting the rush-hour traffic to arrive on time at the plant or office. If this alone is not totally convincing about the bliss of retirement, talk to your former coworkers about the politics, backbiting, work-loads, changes, and shared adversity that you have left behind. If you're still unconvinced, stay at the office until 6:00 p.m., then struggle to get out of the parking lot that is the freeway and arrive home late, to the disapproval of your spouse and ruined plans for the evening. If you still remain nostalgic, you probably should apply for your old job or look for a new one.

THE EMOTIONAL CROSSCURRENTS

All employees develop some sort of an emotional attachment to their jobs. It is often ambivalent—with alternate feelings of both like and dislike—but most people enjoy some aspects of working and many rely on it to support their identity and self-esteem, and to satisfy narcissistic needs. In some instances the rewards and recognition received at work are of such importance that they surface as obstacles to a smooth entry into retirement. Let's explore some of the psychological crosscurrents that can impact the transition.

Feelings of Loss

Emotional support structures built into the work environment often go unnoticed or are taken for granted. Daily contact and interaction often lead to coworkers becoming close friends and confidants. And these relationships tend to disseminate into outside social activities. Likewise, family activities can become intertwined into your work through company outings, business travel, and company-sponsored services such as day care, volunteer work, and community projects.

Working together with a common goal builds a sense of team spirit and unity. In a team environment, collaboration, the challenges of collective problem solving, and shared adversity bring members together. Each work environment has its own rhythm and flow, and in many supportive corporate cultures, there is a sustaining matrix into which employees fit and feel comfortable.

> *Loved ones must realize that a problem with letting go does not take away from how much the retiree loves his or her home and family.*

Retirement means leaving behind these emotional supports and congenial working relationships. However you may catalog the good things about the job—be it influence, responsibility, team-work, camaraderie, friendship, control, passion, or recognition—all employees can identify features of their work that satisfy them. These positive features convey a sense of belonging and self-worth that may be difficult to leave behind. As an unknown ancient Chinese philosopher observed, "In life, the leaving of something is the true appreciation of it." Often you do not fully appreciate the special nature of your workplace until it is gone.

Departure from the firm may trigger a grief reaction complete with denial and depression, but it usually subsides gradually in a similar fashion to other periods of grieving. Loved ones need to understand this psychological response and be patient. They must realize that a problem with letting go does not take away from how much you love your home and family.

Changes of Structure

For the employed, the daily pattern of living is usually structured around the work week. The repetitive day-to-day activities build a deeply embedded routine. The average man or woman works forty or so hours per week, not including thirty to sixty minutes for lunch, the preparation time getting ready for work, and transportation time to and from work. Depending on factors such as how long it takes you to get ready and how far you live from your work, outside considerations for work can claim anywhere from five to twenty additional hours each week.

Work creates boundaries outside the home. The firm has a hierarchy of supervision and a pecking order of responsibility. There are clearly established expectations, and goals are in place to work toward. The firm has a community culture complete with well-established cliques and a social grapevine. Demanding work often appropriates the lion's share of your creative and emotional energies, and the mission of the firm subsumes your individuality.

Consistency, predictability, rhythm, and familiarity are reassuring. Knowing the ropes, understanding boundaries, and knowing what to expect produces a trustworthy structure that combats stress. Many employees thrive on the work routine and seem lost without it. How often have you heard a friend or coworker say, "I'm bored after six to eight days of vacation and look forward to going back to work"?

John Sloan Dickey, a former president of Dartmouth College, had a favorite expression when counseling undergraduate students: "Work keeps at bay boredom, vice, and need." Indeed, work is an occupier that corrals the wayward spirit. Without the organized format of work, activities become more self-directed and reflective of your desires, and your desires alone. This exposes more of your true personality and emotional underpinnings. As a result, the disappearance of the boundaries of employment can unmask and amplify preexisting emotional problems such as mild depression, compulsive behaviors, and suppressed anger. A stable job is no longer there to support the emotional defense mechanisms to compensate for these unresolved conflicts.

"Work keeps at bay boredom, vice, and need."

Being swept up and consumed by work and business matters is a familiar workplace malady. The work ethic and total commitment to the job is still very much alive in America. Medical residents and interns commonly work eighty or more hours per week. Striving business executives carry briefcases home packed with enough homework to make a college student cringe. Endless sweat equity is the *sine qua non* for the thousands of new entrepreneurial start-up ventures. In our society we are taught how to work and not how to play. Unfortunately, many develop a stubborn addiction to the former. With a thirty- to forty-year work history that is highly structured within tight boundaries, how do you learn to enjoy freelance pleasures and freestyle expression?

Many retirees who thrive on structure are advised either to coast into retirement through part-time work or undertake new directions to fill the void. For most, substituting other structured activities such as hobbies, family activities, church work, sports, and similar ventures will suffice. Just make sure to find a way to add some structure to your life.

Redirecting Nervous Energy

Many employees use the work environment to direct their nervous energies and to help soothe emotions raised by the less structured areas of their lives. Maintaining a healthy internal emotional life may depend upon the range of emotional outlets provided by a job. Interestingly, a job that affords adequate opportunities to express these nervous drives often translates into a highly productive work environment with an energetic workforce.

We can cite many examples where a job affords acceptable outlets for emotional release: the construction worker who knocks down buildings; the Army drill instructor who whips the recruits into shape; the surgeon who cuts people open; the exterminator who can purge any pest; the football lineman who collides with reckless abandon into the opposing lineman; and the consummate salesman whose need to be liked is fulfilled with every sale. In most instances, sublimation and overcompensation at work are positive behaviors.

But the workplace can also tolerate negative outlets for aggression: the abusive boss who practices a seagull style of management (flies in, makes lots of noise, defecates, and then flies away); the tactless clerk who vents her angry feelings on the customer; the disgruntled coworker who spreads rumors and gossip. Who has not seen examples of the office bully, the predatory traffic cop, the sly office politician, the crooked manager, and the sadistic supervisor?

Work dissipates and neutralizes highly charged emotions in a variety of ways, positive and negative. When you retire, the expressive outlets at the workplace retire with you, leaving a new burden of emotional expression within the context of new activities.

Assault on Self-Esteem

A job with rich emotional support, rewards, and recognition may compensate for poor self-esteem. From there, it is a simple leap to link personal self-worth with job responsibilities. Our puritan work ethic leads us to believe that relaxation and idleness are akin to laziness and dereliction. This compulsive work ethic tends to associate self-esteem with hard work, results, and other "useful" activities. But to adjust to retirement, the social imperatives and pressures to keep busy and produce must be subdued—you must come to realize that self-esteem is more than a measure of how hard you work.

Self-esteem is also a victim of some other negative connotations associated with retirement. Being "put out to pasture" sounds like you are an inert potted plant, and "growing old" implies decline and weakness. Youth is promulgated as the norm. Unlike many other societies, especially in Asia, ours is not imbued with ancestor worship or great deference to the older living generations. By contrast, our society is mobile, forward looking, trendy, and adaptable to change. The reality that the old order is being replaced by the new order at an accelerating pace offers little consolation to the retiree whose self-esteem is under attack from all sides.

You must come to realize that self-esteem is more than a measure of how hard you work.

For some people, self-esteem is based upon successful competition, adventuresome risk-taking, and a dynamite job. Retirement to a family environment changes the ground rules and increases the need for a different set of skills such as emotional intimacy, trust, companionship, and community. These new requirements may be difficult to accept, learn, and practice, but they are highly supportive of self-esteem. In the long run, these sensitivity skills should provide even greater self-esteem and fulfillment. Enjoy this marvelous opportunity to learn the "warm and fuzzy" skills that enrich life.

Depletion Anxiety

Aging and retirement are reluctant partners but are bonded at all levels of head, heart, and hands. At a base level, life is the process of wearing out gradually. Humans are born with an abundance of resilience within all organ systems. The kidneys are a good example. A normal adult has enough renal function to survive on one quarter of just one kidney. Stated differently, an individual would need to lose about 85 percent of normal kidney function before developing symptoms of renal insufficiency and failure. Similar margins of safety exist for other organ systems including the brain, heart, lungs, and liver.

Experience has significant survival value.

Everyday wear and tear is responsible for the gradual decline of those physiological reserves. These losses occur over many years and produce no symptoms until very late in the process. All body tissues and organ systems are involved, and disease can accelerate the process. The time to heal and recuperate from illness or injury lengthens. Medical conditions such as diabetes, hypertension, obesity, and arteriosclerosis affect multiple organ systems simultaneously.

Fortunately, life's school of experience helps to compensate for this gradual deterioration. Wisdom, position, wealth, and intuition level the playing field and help compensate for some of the physical shortcomings. Learning from mistakes usually helps avoid repeating them and fosters greater common sense. Seniority and ascending the hierarchy in the firm expands the boundaries of influence and control. Accumulated wealth gives options and influence, and a mature intuition—that instinctive inner voice—shepherds your decision making. Experience has significant survival value.

In addition to the normal aging process, we must also consider the rising threat of serious illness. Perhaps Alzheimer's disease, the most common form of slowly progressive dementia, instills more fear about decline than any other disorder. Indeed, "senior moments," when we forget a name, block on the recall of a fact, or lose details when telling a story, are common to all of us and should not raise the specter of Alzheimer's. But as we get older, many of us see a close acquaintance devastated by this disorder, and it can make the threat seem very immediate. Fortunately, medical research for an Alzheimer's cure is highly focused and on track to solve the riddle of this disease. Current statistics show that Alzheimer's disease afflicts 5 percent of persons over the age of seventy and 20–40 percent over the age of eighty-five.

Depletion anxiety is a universal concern about the aging process. Bundled into this category are fear of illness, dying, impotence, ugliness, crippling disease, and senility. Retirement gives you time to reflect upon mortality and to realistically assess how to improve your lifestyle in order to conserve vitality. When querying nonagenarians on the secret of longevity, they usually respond, "Do everything in moderation, and appreciate your limits." And contrary to legend, I know of no nonagenarians who smoke or are morbidly obese.

Free at Last?

Personal freedom is one of the best features of retirement. You no longer have to report to anyone but yourself. The consequences and ripple effect of making mistakes are reduced. You are freed from the monotony of repetitive tasks that define a job description and the occasional tyranny of the powers that be. At last you have free rein to do what you want to do. Interests that have been neglected for decades can be reincarnated; time is yours to sharpen the golf game, refinish furniture, visit local museums, join Kiwanis, etc. For the first time in your life, you have the latitude to set the bar of performance, activity, and accountability at any level you choose.

But after a lifetime of keeping your nose to the grindstone, this freedom can be a source of bewilderment. How do you deal with time on your hands? How do you measure your personal worth when your activities do not give traditional, measurable results? The work ethic does not die easily. How do you convince yourself that you are really free and out from under the yoke of employment?

These forces often drive the new retiree to be hyperactive. We often hear, "I'm busier now than before retirement," and, "There are more things than I have time to do." Such expressions make you wonder why anyone would want to graduate from one excessively busy schedule to another. What about the time set aside to smell the roses?

This period of high intensity may explain why the initial period in retirement is often likened to a honeymoon or the first one hundred days in an elected office. High expectations often stimulate a frenzy of activity as you go about getting caught up on all those projects you saved for retirement. In most instances, a backlog of projects is beneficial to help you transition into the uncharted territory of retirement. It may help to gradually displace the identity as a worker bee and speed the substitution of a new agenda.

However, this initial burst of energy usually is not sustainable. Ultimately you must create a new pattern of living that is in sync with your energy levels, calms your soul, and satisfies the plan that you have created for retirement. You need to give yourself the necessary time to adjust to your newly found freedom and become comfortable with it; only then will you allow yourself to settle down and truly enjoy the spaces between activities.

Allow yourself to settle down and truly enjoy the spaces between activities.

AN OUNCE OF PREVENTION

With retirement comes a major psychological shift. Your purpose and goals are literally turned upside down. It takes time to get your footing and handle the emotional adjustment. Start early with a bit of self-analysis—think about what the workplace means to you to help you anticipate the emotional barriers during the transition. The six psychological forces we have covered are a starting point to assist in your introspection. As with all aspects of retirement, planning and preventative measures can help you immeasurably.

CHAPTER 6

Sexual Intimacy

*R*etirement frees time and energy you can devote to the renewal of intimacy and sexuality. Among older generations, openly discussing sexual matters has always been a bit awkward and inhibited by the taboos of our upbringing. Sex education was rudimentary in high school. Parents often fell short when discussing the "birds and the bees" due to embarrassment and a paucity of accurate information. For many of us, the information we got about sex in our youth was more or less derived from peer hearsay that was skewed by misinformation and boasting. Learning about sex became an on-the-job training exercise, and not infrequently the learning began abruptly on the wedding night.

Today, sexual matters, especially sexual dysfunction and the perfect sexual relationship, are widely discussed in all the media. But many individuals continue to know little about the anatomy, physiology, and psychology of sexual functioning. Additionally, in our society, the need to project an aura of virility is deeply rooted in the male ego, making it difficult for men to reveal problems of a sexual nature and seek medical advice for them.

Medical practices have new tools to help remedy sexual dysfunction and facilitate a new intimacy at almost any age.

Assuming you avoid illegal activities, there are no standards or benchmarks that define what are normal or abnormal sexual behaviors. The definition of normalcy rests within personal expectations, individual preferences, and moral principles. However, some studies suggest that as high as 22 percent of men and 43 percent of women have some problem in the sexual response cycle. For this substantial group there is good news. Medical practices have new tools to help remedy sexual dysfunction and facilitate a new intimacy at almost any age.

MALE ERECTILE DYSFUNCTION

As recently as twenty years ago, this type of problem was largely ignored. Patients who were bold enough to complain were told that treatment was ineffective and they must accept the problems as irreversible. However, today there is a full array of treatments for erectile dysfunction (ED) that have generated a flood of men seeking advice and treatment.

Here are some of the common modalities used by physicians to treat the problem today.

- Vacuum erectile devices (VEDs) in which chambered negative pressure is used to create an erection that is captured with a constricting band at the base of the penis. Despite its mechanical and unnatural characteristics, the VED remains a successful noninvasive alternative.

- Testosterone injections to increase sexual desire. Returning every two to four weeks to the physician's office for an injection has some effect in increasing libido while at the same time reassuring the patient that he is being treated for a medical condition, and that it is not all in his head. In addition, it buys time for situational and interpersonal problems to resolve themselves spontaneously.

- The surgical implantation of semirigid rods or inflatable penile prostheses into the two corporal bodies of the penis. These devices provide an adequate erection on demand to ensure vaginal penetration. The use of penile prostheses is declining as new oral medications become available.

- Needle injection of prostaglandin E and other agents directly into the penis to produce erection. Although very effective, few patients are content to use this technique long-term, and there is a slight risk of priapism, a firm erection that lasts longer than one to two hours. If priapism occurs, it is a true surgical emergency and must be reversed in order to prevent permanent damage to the penis.

- Sexual counseling through individual, couple, or group psychotherapy. Many specialized sexual dysfunction clinics exist that employ traditional counseling, sex education, and even surrogate partners.

- The greatest advancement during the past ten years has been the advent of oral medications that produce erection by causing the release of nitric oxide. These compounds act directly on the penis and genitalia to produce erection and convey to the brain a feeling of sexual arousal. Viagra, Levitra, and Cialis are the proprietary names for the most commonly used drugs for ED on the market today. These pharmaceuticals have been found to be effective in the majority of impotent patients regardless of cause. Absorption of these agents varies, but in general the pill is taken thirty to sixty minutes before intended intercourse, and the effects last for hours. Fortunately, priapism is rarely seen with these medications. They are remarkably safe and effective but are contraindicated in certain types of cardiovascular disease. They also may exhibit adverse side effects when taken with some other types of medications. They should be taken only under the direction of a physician.

The majority of men seeking help will find a suitable remedy using one or more of the methods listed above.

Causes of Impotence in Men

Differentiating organic (disease-related) and psychogenic (emotionally related) erectile dysfunction has always been a challenge for clinicians. Most studies using standardized psychological and physiological testing fail to show consistent results that accurately define purely organic or purely psychogenic impotence. The problem in most patients has a mixed cause.

Investigators have identified many diseases that contribute to impotence. In general, male patients are relieved to be told their problem relates to an illness and not to an emotional problem or neurosis. Performance anxiety, the worry about achieving an erection, always becomes a factor in persisting erectile problems. To be given a tangible medical explanation for the problem that can be shared with the mate takes away the burden of masculine self-control and the implied guilt of "you just don't love me like you used to."

In the small percentage of patients diagnosed with straightforward psychogenic erectile dysfunction, psychotherapy and counseling are generally the initial treatment of choice. But working through sexual problems with counseling is time-consuming and expensive, and although the short-term results are usually promising, the long-term outcomes are disappointing. Health insurance rarely pays for counseling. Consequently, most treatments for erectile failure, even if it is psychogenic in origin, gravitate toward medication and more mechanical interventions.

Although many medical problems may preexist, the vast majority of sexual dysfunction problems have situational and psychological components. Sexual functioning is central to human survival, and it is a physiological function that is quite durable and fail-safe. Most men retain potency into old age, and the old adage, "If you use it, you won't lose it" rings true. But unfortunately, sexual prowess and multiple orgasms become defectors in middle age. The physical experience of sex becomes more a matter of comfort and mutual gratification than speed, ecstasy, and passion.

A host of conditions associated with aging hinder sexual activity. Heart disease, high blood pressure, diabetes, arthritis, female menopause, depression, lower testosterone levels, and marital indifference are a few of the common denominators. An old expression states that in younger men, sexual functioning is 90 percent physical and 10 percent mental, whereas in older men it is 10 percent physical and 90 percent mental. This may seem to be a debatable generalization, but clinical observations suggest it is not far from the truth.

Prostate Cancer

Prostate cancer warrants special attention. According to the American Cancer Society, in 2007 there were 218,890 men diagnosed with prostate cancer and an estimated 27,000 died from the disease, second only to lung cancer as the leading cause of death in males. Autopsy studies show that 20 percent of men age fifty, and greater than 70 percent of men age eighty, have microscopic or tiny areas of prostate cancer. The overriding problem for the clinician is that there is no sure way to differentiate between the benign tumors and those that will progress. Moreover, except in a limited group of younger patients with a life expectancy in excess of ten years, there is no survival advantage to aggressive treatment for prostate cancer. Aggressive treatments include total surgical removal of the prostate, implantation of radioactive seeds into it, and external beam irradiation. When aggressive intervention is recommended, the patient is well advised to seek multiple opinions and research the subject. Although prostate cancer rarely initiates sexual dysfunction, the treatments for this disorder may cause it.

FEMALE SEXUAL DYSFUNCTION

Fewer women seek medical counsel specifically for sexual dysfunction than men, so no valid statistics exist that clearly document the differences in this problem's occurrence between the genders. (Interestingly, about half the men seen for impotence have been encouraged by their frustrated female partners to seek medical advice.) Obviously, the absence of a performance measure like male erection means female sexual dysfunction may be more easily concealed or even go unrecognized. Medical evaluation and treatment for female sexual dysfunction has only recently drawn widespread attention in scientific literature and the media.

Obstetricians/gynecologists often provide continuing general medical care to women throughout their reproductive years and into post-menopausal life. Consequently, they often enjoy the trust of a long-term relationship. This makes for easy, open discussion of sexual matters. In recent years, medical science has provided new insights into the nature and treatment for lack of erotic response (frigidity) and female orgasmic dysfunction. And it appears that, just as in the male, new medications, some of which are considered "lifestyle," will be used to treat these problems.

Menopause can affect a woman's self-image and sexual functioning. The decline in estrogen and testosterone levels often causes a decline in the interest and ability for arousal. Hormone Replacement Therapy (HRT) with estrogen and progesterone has historically been used to postpone or reverse menopausal symptoms and the physical effects of menopause. However, in August 2002, a study of 16,608 women taking HRT by the Women's Health Initiative/ the National Institute of Health revealed significant risks for women on long-term HRT. It showed significantly increased risks of breast cancer, heart disease, stroke, and blood-clot problems. The study did also show a decrease in hip fractures from osteoporosis and a lower incidence of colorectal cancer. In view of these findings that are currently under critical review, it is recommended that all women take HRT only under the close supervision of a doctor.

The Differences between Male and Female Sexual Response

There are obvious differences between the male and female anatomy. However, there are some common—yet debatable and imprecise—generalizations about the differences in sexual response and responsiveness. (For more on this topic, Appendix A contains a bibliography of resource books that explore contemporary issues and encompass current thinking about the entire subject of human sexuality.)

In the process of sexual arousal and searching for a mate, men and women place different value on physical characteristics, personality traits, and affluence. Men seem to be more enticed by visual images such as physical attractiveness and seductive behavior. Indeed, studies have shown that viewing pornographic film clips produces greater response in men than in women. On the other hand, women are attracted to handsome men but also look beyond physical appearance to security and safety issues. To women, power, influence, and financial shelter are sexy and attractive male qualities. This framework has been known to result in fusing the male's desire for a dazzling partner into a woman's desire for safe relationships. The "trophy wife" is well known in the circles of power and influence.

Males have external plumbing. By the time puberty is at hand and wet dreams occur, the male has already researched the power of this male genital organ. After all, most boys have been self-experimenting with this prized protrusion since early childhood.

In women, the discovery process is not so easy. To visually inspect their external genital organs, they need a mirror. Engorgement does occur just like in the male, but not to the same degree as in the erect penis. Also, in general, society is more tolerant of masturbation in boys than it is in girls. You could say that from every perspective, sex is more hidden for the young woman than the man and that learning about sexuality is more complicated.

Recent studies have also shown that a lack of sexual activity in men causes a definable increase in the desire for sexual activity. In women, no such time-related increase in desire was measurable. With regard to sexual arousal, men seem to be sprinters and self-starters, whereas women need contact and a process to get into the mood.

PSYCHOLOGICAL INFLUENCES ON SEXUAL SATISFACTION

The quality of human sexual response in both men and women depends upon many factors and circumstances. Relationships are never static, and no year is exactly like the one before it. Sexual functioning changes during the autumn years of life due to the social, psychological, and physical processes that come into play. These processes can produce unhealthy and damaging changes as well as healthy adjustments and patterns. Four of these common changes are discussed below.

1. Sexual Fantasy and Partner Idealization

In a Darwinian framework, mating is a highly selective process. The alpha male is determined by male superiority and dominance, which wins him access to breeding partners. Females are innately drawn to the most powerful male.

Traditional psychology holds that, subconsciously, girls tend to seek mates who resemble their fathers, and boys seek mates who resemble their mothers. To a child, the parent of the opposite sex is often idealized and put on a pedestal. This is a natural result of a bonded relationship with a capable and seemingly all-powerful parent. The fantasies attached to a parent evolve in childhood when the father or mother is young and vital and the center of the youngster's universe. Thus a mental model of the ideal person or mate is molded by an image of excellence.

A reinforcement process occurs in adolescence. Social norms and peer perceptions idealize the opposite sex. The attractive male is characterized as influential, strong, and confident; the popular female is attractive, outgoing, and fit. This superlative image is diffused into the sexual fantasy world of both sexes.

On top of that, day to day throughout our lives we are inundated with a contemporary culture that markets idealization. The media and promotional industry worship at the altar of youth, beauty, and athleticism. Sexual innuendo and seduction are pervasive. The featured athletes are young and brawny; the models are impossibly slim, young, and lovely. This milieu of hype, spin, and excessive stimulation fosters unrealistic expectations. Moreover, the sexual overload produces a type of insensitivity and numbness that diffuses sexual energies. This may make it more difficult to refocus them on your partner.

Our culture often makes men and women feel they are being shortchanged by being married to ordinary people who do not necessarily improve with age. With time, surface beauty is supplanted by wrinkles, cellulite, gray hair, and hair that grows in the wrong places. Strenuous activity seems more demanding and tiring. Increased fat deposits create a new body contour. Sleep patterns change; snoring and insomnia are more common. The natural aging process alters libido and body image.

How do you reconcile these imaginary and idealized expectations with reality? Marriage has been defined as the "epitome of tolerance." Aging raises the bar of tolerance, requiring one to mentally rework expectations and develop a deeper, more empathetic understanding of the time of life. Sexual gratification becomes increasingly linked to your ability to emotionally adjust to the changes of age and the unrealistic expectations fostered by the media.

2. Alteration in the Sexual Experience

For men, the intensity and quality of the orgasm diminishes with aging. Often this occurs so gradually that it goes unnoticed. The male orgasmic experience, or cascade, has two distinct parts. The first event is emission, which produces the most intense sensation. This occurs when the muscle of the bladder neck and urethral sphincter contract to create a high-pressure chamber within the prostate gland. The second event is the rhythmic contractions of the pelvic muscles that produce ejaculation. Although a gradual decrease in the volume of the ejaculate occurs, the intensity of the sensation with ejaculation changes little with advancing age. But prostate problems and functional changes eventually have a profound impact on the quality of the sensation.

Also, as a man ages, the duration of the refractory period—the interval before he can start again after orgasm—increases, and lovemaking through multiple orgasms becomes less possible. Additionally, the degree of friction and length of stimulation required to produce and maintain an erection and produce an orgasm increases with age. The requirements for physical and mental stamina increase proportionately. To top things off, lowered serum testosterone levels undermine the fervent sex drive.

With this background, it is apparent that determination and tenacity, plus a focus of emotional resources, are necessary if the excitement of sexual pursuit in a timeworn relationship is to be maintained. Fortunately, the intimacy and better understanding within a proven relationship help to compensate for changing physical expression.

3. Conditioned Behavior

Sexual functioning depends upon complex chemical changes in the brain. Dopamine, serotonin, oxytocin, vasopressin, and endogenous opioids are neurotransmitter substances whose concentrations change and usually increase with the progression of sexual activity. Recent work using brain scanning techniques show the area of the brain active in sexual activity to be the same as the one that produces the euphoria induced by drugs. This suggests that sexual activity may involve the same part of the brain that is associated with drug addiction. The wild exhilaration and infatuation of love is certainly consistent with addictive, obsessive-compulsive, and highly conditioned behavior.

The physiological changes that occur during intercourse for both men and women are mediated and controlled by the autonomic (sympathetic), or involuntary, nervous system. Neurotransmitter molecules act on specific nerve cells to produce penile erection, clitoral engorgement, and orgasm. Unlike a voluntary action such as moving your legs or arms, your brain cannot command an erection or female arousal to occur without simultaneously mobilizing sexual desire. Both male erection and female sexual excitement hinge upon the desire and cannot easily be forced, faked, or manufactured. Lacking an organic or psychogenic cause for erectile failure or frigidity, sexual response is a reliable barometer of the sexual attraction that exists in a relationship.

Sexual functioning is a highly conditioned behavior that is acutely sensitive to positive and negative reinforcement. Once a stable, gratifying pattern of sexuality with a partner is established, it tends toward consistency—a repetitive behavior that becomes hard-wired and imprinted in the brain. The success, intimacy, and repeated positive reinforcement of sexual gratification give it an addictive property. On the other hand, just like any violation of trust, one or two bad experiences can turn off the eager sexual response.

Sexual fantasy and creative idiosyncrasy play an important role in sexual conditioning and response. Fantasy can be revisited and reinvented throughout the years of a relationship. Couples with a good sexual adjustment tend to carry it well into middle age and beyond.

4. Sexual Incompatibility

Much has been written about the chemistry of love, romantic infatuation, and sexual attraction. Scientific study of these phenomena has produced no clear conclusive results. Pheromones and odor, body language, timing, proximity, and the Freudian search for a parent may all play roles in our choice of mate, roles that we can't measure. Sexual feeling and gratification is also always subjective. Physical signs that signal sexual receptivity vary, and some researchers even suggest that each of us develops a "love map" that acts as a blueprint for what we consider attractive. This may explain why some people tend to pursue and marry the same type of partner over and over again even when it has previously been a formula for failure.

Each partner responds to unique sets of messages and interprets flirtation differently. With so many differences, it is not unusual to find sexual dysfunction that is partner-specific. Indeed, many marriages are highly functional even as the partners live as sexual strangers.

Practical Activities for a Better Sex Life

- Plan time alone together in complete privacy, without any distractions.

- Be a little experimental and try new things such as wearing provocative lingerie or playing out a mutually arousing fantasy.

- Open up, and let your partner know what pleases you. Discuss preferences.

- Maintain a sense of humor; if things don't pan out, you can always return another day. Laughter often is the best lubricant.

- Carry romance and courtship outside the bedroom, and make it a part of everyday activities.

- Leave anger and disappointments from the past in the past. Forgive easily, and view your relationship as a renewal process each day.

- Stay positive and constructive. Criticism never made anyone a better lover.

KEEP TALKING

Regardless of medical science and the psychological underpinnings within the marriage, the best predictor of sexual intimacy is open communication between the partners. However, for older generations it may still be embarrassing to be candid about these sensitive issues, even after decades of marriage. Explicit sex education, pornography in the media, and open discussion about orgasms and sexual needs were not a part of the culture when we were growing up. But it is never too late to become a student and begin the dialogue and learning process.

The best predictor of sexual intimacy is open communication between the partners.

How often have you heard someone say, "You only live once"? How often have you looked back and reflected on the chances and opportunities you let go by? Now is the time to take the risk to express your sexual needs to your partner and indicate your commitment to do what is necessary to rekindle the fires. What you do in the bedroom is private. Dirty movies, sexy language, erotic role-playing, medical enhancements, oils, vibrators, and so on are not signs of perversion but rather creative sexual play. Relish the thought that your grandchildren might be stunned and even disapprove.

Relish the thought that your grandchildren might be stunned and even disapprove.

The bottom line is that the motivation of a couple to confront and solve any problem with sexual dysfunction is more important to the outcome than whether the problem is related to organic or psychogenic causes. It takes two to do the tango of sexual intimacy, and both partners must be unselfish in working together. If this fails to produce results, be reassured that medical science has the tools to further evaluate and resolve the problem for a highly motivated couple.

★ CHAPTER 7 ★
Spending Some Time Alone

*M*ost retirees face an increased amount of time alone. With the natural narrowing of life's social orbit—no longer going to an office full of people—you generally interact with fewer people on a day-to-day basis. Unlike the scheduled workflow of employment, your retirement agenda has empty slots and possibly even some blank pages. With more than thirty years of experience working fifty to seventy hours a week, to ponder what you're going to do with your day may seem a bit strange and unfamiliar. Never before have your personal interests been called upon to fill your entire schedule rather than just the weekends and holidays. It's a new playing field that is welcome, but like any new situation, it can be fraught with uneasiness.

Once you retire, a lot of the peak times for the activities that you enjoy fall during the weekday, when many of your buddies are at work. It may be more difficult to recruit them for shared activities and take more effort to organize group outings. Tennis matches will have to be scheduled at 5:00 p.m. or later, and foursomes for competitive golf usually firm up only on Saturdays or an afternoon when you can arrange for the others to take time away from work. A whole range of social gatherings and committee obligations cannot be shifted to a daytime framework and require evening meetings. This includes poker and bridge games as well as the meetings of social clubs and civic organizations.

But most people need a daily infusion of social stimulation to remain vital, and with the mandatory interaction of work gone, this likely involves some planning.

Here's where some forethought can help to solve this problem. As mentioned in Chapter 1, before you retire, try to work on cultivating a broader network of friends and acquaintances with interests similar to yours. Concentrate on those who have ample free time because they are retired, work only part-time, or have a flexible schedule.

However, the central issue here revolves around how you feel about solitary activities. Many people prefer being alone and actually limit social activities. And being content to amuse yourself has its advantages. But most people need a daily infusion of social stimulation to remain vital, and with the mandatory interaction of work gone, this likely involves some planning.

THE NEW SCHEDULE

In retirement, a new schedule evolves over time—it does not present itself immediately when you get your gold watch. Individuals who do not rush to repopulate their time commitments generally make wiser choices in finding fulfilling activities, and not just activities that fill time.

If you can amuse yourself with the simple pleasures that are close at hand, you have taken a giant step toward vanquishing the distress of being alone and having nothing to do.

First, you have no obligation to be fully engaged in retirement. Test the waters first. Try to expand your simple pleasures to occupy your free time. Learn to savor the sounds of silence. Those who keep running without slowing the pace often overlook some of the greatest pleasures of this time. Be self-indulgent and introspective. Why wake with the alarm clock set at seven when you can gently awaken two hours later, after the last pleasant cycle of REM sleep? Why not take yourself to a matinee in the afternoon or peruse those dusty, unread books that clutter the bookcases? A leisurely stroll through the neighborhood to admire the homes and get to know your neighbors and their children is often rewarded with new friendships and neighborhood news. If you can amuse yourself with the simple pleasures that are close at hand, you have taken a giant step toward vanquishing the distress of being alone and having nothing to do.

Being a Soloist

Many people choose to live alone without committed partners or long-term stable relationships. For some individuals this independence generates a sense of freedom, autonomy, and creativity. Indeed, in recent years we are seeing greater numbers of soloists who seem content and even happier to live alone.

There are many more women living alone than men. The average woman lives approximately five years longer than the average man does. Although at birth the number of male babies outnumbers female babies, this ratio reverses during early adult life due to a predominance of male premature death related to suicide, work injuries, violent crime, smoking, and auto accidents. Men also tend to marry women younger than they are by one or more years, and when they divorce and remarry, the age difference between the partners skyrockets. This results in a host of relatively young women who must face an extended period alone after the husband passes on.

The female spouse, when fortified with the knowledge that in all probability she will outlive her husband, should prepare to confront this tragedy. And she should ask questions about her future situation and begin to consider an emotional survival plan.

Men are not as tough as women when it comes to being alone.

Men do not do as well living alone. If divorced or widowed, they remarry at a much higher rate than women. Surveys of divorced men and women reveal that a higher percentage of men wish to remarry and are actively seeking new partners. Furthermore, statistics show a significant decrease in life expectancy for men who are single. Men are not as tough as women when it comes to being alone.

Within most people there exists a fundamental need and desire to share the journey of life. Unfortunately, the caprice of life leaves many people without options to meet this need that assumes increasing importance with retirement and advancing age. Misfortune is often unavoidable. But most of the time, you can take charge of your destiny and make things happen. The remainder of this chapter offers practical ideas to rectify the dilemma of being alone.

HAPPY SOLO LIVING

Many individuals who marry, raise children, and thrive in a bustling household have only marginal experience and negligible survival training in living alone. After the loss of a mate, the silence and chill in an empty nest is an alien and disheartening experience. It may cushion the emotional insult when your children live close by, and you have grandchildren to animate your home. However, it is unlikely that your progeny can be a complete surrogate for the security, solace, and constancy of a life partner.

Your outlook and perceptions can be the sole reason for loneliness. Feelings of indifference and withdrawal, even when you are in a crowd of people, are a universal experience for all of us from time to time. Depression, fatigue, stress, anxiety, senility, and debility all contribute to and can be responsible for unrelenting feelings of being lost and alone. And being chronically downbeat with the ones you love can ultimately drive them away and increase your time alone.

At some time in life, most of us will need to deal with a period alone due to the loss of a partner or some other tragedy, and we must cope with the newfound loneliness and solitude. Catastrophic loss of a mate usually produces an overwhelming grief that spans many months or even years; it replaces all sense of purpose and meaning to life with overwhelming feelings of sadness and hopelessness. But time and patience are a reliable cure for grief, and over time, you will gain the strength to again grasp control of the rudder and go on with your life.

The Power of Pets

Recent studies have shown that animals are a remarkably positive tonic for lonely people. This is especially true for the disabled or those living in assisted living or nursing homes. With just a periodic visit with a dog or a cat, studies confirm an improved attitude and responsiveness among nursing-home residents. It appears that the affection and physical contact from warm and fuzzy creatures has genuine therapeutic value. Indeed, the many billions spent on domestic animal care each year attests to the humanization of pets almost to "people" status.

FINDING A MATE IN THE GOLDEN YEARS

If you wish to settle down with a new partner post-retirement, you must adopt a positive mind-set and personally assume the responsibility to make your search for that new special someone successful. Prime the motivational pump, and plan your efforts to connect. Without question, there are emotional risks to being aggressive, and you must be willing to take a chance and be somewhat vulnerable to the loss of pride and embarrassment that can come with unrequited flirtation and affection. But the rewards can be great. And to use a metaphor, it is like selling a house: You only need the commitment from one qualified buyer. It usually doesn't happen by chance but rather by design. During the search you may need to draw upon your religious spirituality to supply courage and single-minded toughness. Not surprisingly, the new partner with a similar need is often found at a church function.

> *You must be willing to take a chance and be somewhat vulnerable to the loss of pride and embarrassment that can come with unrequited flirtation and affection.*

Hurdles and Self-Assessment

But the statistics are not always in your favor. The arrival at middle age makes finding a suitable new mate more difficult. This is especially true for women, since their greater life expectancy makes them more numerous than men, and eligible men often marry younger women. Moreover, men and women alike become less docile and malleable with age. Often, likes and dislikes crystallize and embed in personalities. Moreover, past experience can come with the baggage of pain and disappointments that bring a myriad of negative transferences. Consequently, life's veterans can be very picky and judgmental.

Another hurdle to remarriage are meddlesome children and step-children. A second or third marriage, even if carefully orchestrated with proper protocol and due diligence, is more often than not viewed as a serious threat to the original family's unity, disbursements, and relationships. Either privately or openly, most family members are not shy about voicing their concerns. As is common in our society today, delayed childbearing and the disparity in age between male and female partners in a second marriage also complicate the merging of families.

Moreover, the loss of a mate carries a residual pain that may be so horrendous that it discourages any thoughts of a new serious relationship. In middle age, dating and courtship is a new game again, one that takes courage and chutzpah. And getting started is usually clouded with anxiety. All things considered, it is not surprising that many elect to avoid the hassle and remain alone.

Seizing the Opportunity: Seven Guidelines for Success

For a retired man or woman to find a new life partner is a daunting task. Forming a new permanent relationship is usually undertaken with a degree of caution. And while writing a script to help ensnare a new partner may seem too cold, calculating, and even devious, having a plan produces a much higher success rate than idly standing by and drifting in the pond of limited prospects. Here are seven steps you can take to proactively find a new mate.

*Happenstance, timing, and blind luck
are the rules of the dating game.*

1. **Be motivated.** As mentioned before, you need to be motivated to shoulder the overriding responsibility of making things happen. Friends and acquaintances may "deliver" suitable prospects and facilitate introductions, but they can't begin to understand your special chemistry or needs.

2. **Network.** You must actively put forth the effort to meet and network with as many new people as possible and be prepared to endure the emotional fatigue that is a part of socializing with a new crowd. Keep in mind that referral from your friends and relatives, or even casual acquaintances, often serendipitously opens the doors to a new relationship. Happenstance, timing, and blind luck are the rules of the dating game.

3. **Remember: You are not the only one.** You must appreciate and be convinced of the fact that you are not alone in your quest. Regardless of what others may say and how frustrated you have been in the past, you have lots of company and prospects. Many fine individuals, both male and female, share your predicament and are searching for that special someone. Just searching the hundreds of matchmaking websites that list potential mates of both sexes will quickly confirm this for you.

4. **Use your existing contacts and, possibly, the Internet.** You can leverage your religious, civic, educational, and sporting affiliations. These social activities provide a platform to mix and meet other available men and women. Also, Internet dating and matchmaking has come of age and boasts a reasonable success rate even for senior men and women. But still, most potential new partners reside in your social circles and community.

5. **Keep up appearances.** You should put forth effort to maintain your physical attractiveness and hone your social skills. Remember, first impressions are often lasting ones.

6. **Seek new activities.** Consider pursuing new interests that are widely shared within your targeted group.

7. **Recover first.** If you are in the grieving process, suspend any decision making until you have recovered from the emotional roller coaster. Go slowly with any new commitments.

Once there's a plan in place, you'll likely find that the social interaction of the senior courting game can be invigorating and fun.

ALTERNATIVES TO COUPLING UP

You might feel no need to focus on finding a new mate—maybe you feel that your children, grandchildren, and good friends are more than enough. You may also feel no desire to assume new responsibilities to love and care for another senior citizen. There is no correct answer to the question of loneliness in retirement. It is comforting to be able to rely on the omnipresence of someone who is there primarily for you, but it's not the only way to find happiness and satisfaction.

But being alone can be anyone's destiny—and there's absolutely nothing wrong or shameful about it, whether by design or happenstance. It does not end your chances for a satisfying retirement, nor does it mitigate your self-worth. Pets, children, friends, and family give you someone to reach out and touch when you need it, and security guards, panic buttons, and cell phones can ensure that you're never far from help when you need it. It does take more than a bit of getting used to, and you'll need courage to express your solitary identity and independence, but as with everything in retirement, just plan and prepare, and you'll learn how to make yourself happy.

SECTION III:

Family

CHAPTER 8

Drawing on Family Support

*N*othing has seen more profound change over the past several decades than the American family. New census data shows that traditional two-parent families constitute only 23.5 percent of all U.S. households. This is down from 30.25 percent in 1980. And data for 2003 show that one third of men and one quarter of women between the ages of thirty and thirty-four have never been married, nearly four times the rates in 1970. Almost half of first marriages and 60 percent of remarriages end in divorce. Cohabitation outside of marriage or leading up to marriage is close to the norm. Although the statistics are trending downward, a high percentage of youngsters are sexually active in high school and a high but declining rate of teenage pregnancy persists. Single parents and latchkey kids can be found in virtually all communities and across all socioeconomic strata.

Due to the greater life expectancy of women, there are approximately three widows to every widower. After the loss of a mate, men are seven times more likely to remarry. Birth rates have been comparatively low following the surge of baby-boomers in the 1940s and 50s, and this has resulted in the graying of America. More women are having children later in their reproductive years due to careers, effective birth control and family planning methods, and later marriage. New treatments for infertility aid women in pushing the limits of their biologic clocks.

Though there is no standard definition, the American family is still resilient and remains the cornerstone of American life.

By necessity, most contemporary families have two breadwinners. The Bureau of Labor Statistics indicates that 73 percent of mothers work outside the home. The majority of young American families save less than 2 percent of earnings for retirement and rely exclusively on the equity in their home and company-sponsored retirement plan. In these instances, few financial supports exist in the event of termination, accidents, catastrophic illness, or family emergencies.

The extended family construct of the past has been eroded by the geographic mobility in our society. Many people relocate to other parts of the country for job opportunities and business transfers, the locations of colleges and training programs, the community where in-laws reside, or a climate that supports a particular activity such as skiing and surfing. Because of this, a visit to see all of the grandchildren can require several trips to multiple destinations.

The family has changed by historical measures. The true extended family of a bygone era has disappeared, and increasingly, successive generations tend to scatter and go their separate ways all over the country and beyond. Dependence bonds are shed at an earlier age, and the devotion to family has in part shifted to support systems outside the family. The family circle has shrunk in size. However, even though there is no standard definition, the American family is still resilient and remains the cornerstone of American life.

COMING HOME

Even before retirement, your family knows all about the real you. They are keenly aware of your view of the world and your idiosyncrasies. They know how to push your full keyboard of buttons to provoke most any response. Family involvement before retirement is tempered by multiple escape routes into work responsibilities, but after retirement you are less insulated from family interaction and relationships. To integrate into the home environment and maintain equilibrium after retirement requires a greater emphasis on sharing, tolerance, and accommodation. Discussion and gentle persuasion must prevail; your wishes and desires are better received if they take into account the collective needs of the family.

Families share implied mutual goals and interests that are not too different from a mission statement.

But there are many good reasons to implement these compromises—quality time with family in retirement offers opportunity. It can provide for a heightened openness and ability to express genuine feelings and carry through a dialogue that leads to greater closeness, sharing, and understanding. A stable, functional family support system is a positive predictor of a successful transition into retirement. This is especially true because unlike many milestones, retirement is not just a fork in the road; for most of us it is a relatively irrevocable change in direction that can close many doors that may previously have been open. An expanded, happy family life can lead to a smooth walk down the road of retirement.

Every family is a microcosm of unique cultural characteristics. Precious memories, curious personality traits, particular ways of doing things, and inside jokes color all family relationships. And families share implied mutual goals and interests that are not too different from a mission statement. When retirement comes around, most families have accumulated a backlog of projects to engage the freed energies of the newly retired member. These activities can form a sense of continuity much like the community fostered by the demands of the workplace. Becoming collaborative with other family members can help you transition to retirement in a number of ways.

THE NEW WORK MODEL

Over time all families develop a division of responsibilities and duties. For instance, maybe the wife is responsible for the cooking and taking out the garbage, while the husband washes the dishes and does the yard work. But a distinct reshuffling of these duties can occur following retirement. For instance, with the time that comes from retirement, maybe the male retiree wants to test out his gourmet cooking skills, while the female retiree would like to try her hand at landscaping. If one spouse retires before the other, the retired spouse may take over all the household duties. These rearrangements in interests may change the family dynamic, and if both the man and the woman retire simultaneously it becomes even more challenging.

This realignment invariably leads to some encroachment upon your spouse's territory. Your presence may disrupt some important activities that have previously formed the basis for their copacetic daily routine. This requires accommodation to ensure that both partners have adequate space in which to pursue their individual needs.

Having a repertoire of independent activities usually enhances the quality time you spend together.

Both the partners and the relationship usually benefit when each person expresses a degree of independence within the relationship. A perception of freedom always gives a person the perception of voluntary action. And the more autonomous you feel, the less apt you are to resent any feelings of over-dependence you may have and more likely to freely give the understanding that is central to any enduring relationship. Since overdosing on togetherness in retirement is more common than under-dosing, it is usually wise for a retiree to disrupt the partner's routine as little as possible. Moreover, having a repertoire of independent activities usually enhances the quality time you spend together.

Having the spouse home all day with free time, "in the way" or "making demands" on your attention, may be nerve-wracking and disquieting to the former sanctity of home routine. And the retiree with extra free time may notice a greater tendency to pry into the affairs of family members and offer unasked-for advice. If this becomes too intrusive, it may cause dissension and mutiny. It is best to tend your own store and understand that at the end of the day, you are responsible for your happiness and yours alone, and retirement does not empower you to be the judge in offering the final solutions to all family problems.

REHABILITATING RELATIONSHIPS

Over many years of marriage, interactions tend to become programmed and worn, and the stability within the family is increasingly built on predictability and well-established family paradigms. Often, the demands of child rearing, a full schedule of social activities for both you and your children, and careers preempt any real discussion about transforming relationships. For most people, it is often so difficult just to keep their head above water and meet the immediate demands that they rarely have the energy to even think about ways to create a stronger relationship.

Life carries us along a circuitous route that opens some doors as it closes others. The sacrifices we make for education, marriage, childbearing, careers, family obligations, and aspirations often preempt other goals. Factors such as serendipity, duty, chance, and betrayal also come into play to limit your options through the years. Any one person's life journey has these kinds of regrets, decisions, and sacrifices, and there is no ordinary or stereotypical life.

There is always a tendency to assume in a stable relationship or long-term marriage that we intuitively know what the other is thinking and feeling, but though we may have been next to them through their life story, we weren't living it. Compounding the mystery, each of us has a certain side that we're careful to show others, while keeping other parts of our personality hidden—even from our families. To avoid conflict, we often follow a politically correct rhetoric and maintain a supportive attitude in order to keep the peace. But all these extremely personal experiences and things we always try to keep hidden from other people add up to us never knowing our significant others like we think we do.

Most of us have a somewhat skewed and idealized image of our mate when we first marry. Also, at the start, sexual energies can smooth out most disagreements and one another's occasionally frustrating idiosyncrasies. But after this period of excitement and acceptance, accommodations are made in the majority of marriages that result in harmonious calm. Most individuals genuinely like being married. But over the years personalities do change. Values and interests can diverge, and unresolved anger from either inner conflict or scars from earlier events can act as a barrier to a vibrant alliance.

With the help of your loved ones, a level of intimate comfort and security can be the ultimate reward of a long marriage.

But even if some of the earlier shine may become dull and slightly tarnished, a married couple usually holds onto the essence of a solid and rewarding relationship. We all harbor a special need for the shelter that home provides and the core values embodied in home and family. With the help of your loved ones, a level of intimate comfort and security can be the ultimate reward of a long marriage.

Retirement brings the realization that one has entered the autumn of life. There are no more rungs on the corporate ladder to climb, and your job skills are no longer constantly evaluated. Against this background, it is usually comforting to settle into a day-in, day-out family routine. And retirement is an opportune time to reappraise and even constructively change family paradigms. It's time to begin the open dialogue and consider compromises that make the second half of life just as rewarding, if not more so, than the first.

It is difficult to fundamentally change people or marriages, and retirement rarely provides any instant magic tonic to make families get along perfectly. Major dysfunction within any family tends to linger and resist resolution. But if one brings experience coupled with their best efforts to the table, it often can provide a platform for renewal and change. Retirement offers the opportunity to clear the air. You may have nowhere else to go but home, and this, by itself, is a strong incentive to drive the change process.

Clearing the Air

Retirement affords an excellent window of opportunity to remake primary relationships. To clear the air, a good first step is to forgive your mate unconditionally for all the shortcomings of the past. Recognize any emotional baggage as irrelevant. Likewise, try to sort out, understand, and mitigate the use of negative hot buttons that were used historically in your relationship to get even, have your way, and express anger.

Recognize any emotional baggage as irrelevant.

Psychological tests confirm that spouses frequently harbor distorted impressions about each other's beliefs, perceptions, and motivations. Obviously, some suppressed feelings and conflicting interests can color your relationships, and when these are deep-seated they can present hurdles to major or even minor improvements in that relationship. Consequently, when reformatting your relationship, you must first try to understand this background noise and agree to let bygones be bygones. Fight fair by taking the emotional triggers out of play. Try to address only objective, fixable, relevant, and here-and-now matters that have a place in present and future reality. Make the playing field level.

Recent books written about negotiating skills stress the need to avoid "taking positions," and maintain that all common-interest issues on the table are negotiable and amenable to a mutually satisfactory result—a win-win outcome. Success in life has always equated to compromise, and successful life partners are usually adept at making trade-offs. Certainly, one of the keys to achieving interpersonal change is the avoidance of overbearing command-and-control decrees that in most instances will shut down any evolutionary process. An open mind and flexibility are invaluable.

Men and women usually have different styles of expression and connecting. Men are more accustomed to an aggressive debating format, while women tend to try to achieve consensus and avoid direct confrontation. Women generally smile more frequently and offer positive reinforcement of the other's viewpoint, while men are usually in it to "win." This can add another dimension of miscommunication in an already strained relationship.

Few couples set aside dedicated time to formally discuss interpersonal differences and feelings, or evolve a clear consensus as to where retirement can lead and how they can change to make it better. Too often retirement is a reactive rather than proactive state, and this leaves the transition bobbing on a sea of options and a worn matrix of family paradigms instead of sailing toward a goal that satisfies everyone involved.

> *As strange as it may seem, you often discover new things about your mate that had never occurred to you before.*

Actively discussing and planning your retirement in detail with your mate provides real help from a number of vantage points that go well beyond just financial matters. As strange as it may seem, you often discover new things about your mate that had never occurred to you before. Retirement may expose a greater degree of commonality in interests than you previously appreciated. Why not craft an action plan to improve and guide this new understanding and intimacy?

Writing Your Action Plan

Many retirement books offer lengthy questionnaires to extract information in order to make an assessment of your readiness to retire. Some include questions for the spouse to answer, but in general the exercise is one-sided and overly concrete. It neither buttresses real relationship change nor provides a format for a joint planning exercise.

I prefer a less sterile and loosely structured approach to changing family paradigms. My advice is to have the husband and wife collaborate to produce a logical and methodical plan for change. The process is as follows.

- Initially, each partner independently writes a memorandum to the other. This should be crafted to put forth a complete summary of expectations and new horizons in retirement. The following subjective questions can be used to frame most of the major topics.

  How will retirement alter our home life and that of our extended family?

  How can we integrate our new activities with the old?

  How much time and space does each of us need?

  Will our standard of living need to be lowered, and if so, how do we share the sacrifices that must be made?

  How will retirement affect the composition of our circle of friends and influence our social life?

  How can we build on the strengths within our marriage to meet the increased dependence on domestic activities?

  How do we carry out our obligations to our parents if they become disabled?

What further financial and other assistance might our sons and daughters and their families need, and what is our comfort level with giving this support?

> Scan your mind for at least five new activities that might add zest to your life and your marriage. Write down and review the pros and cons of each.

> List all the reasons why you are looking forward to your partner's retirement.

- After you have let your ideas ferment and made insightful edits to your memorandum, exchange memos with your partner. After you both have had time to read and ponder the other's memo, set aside time for a discussion of your initial impressions and preliminary feedback. At this time, develop one inclusive list of items that might be considered for discussion at a later date.

- Individually prioritize and rate the items on the inclusive list. Then, set aside a time to discuss and cull the list. Those items that make the cut are then considered the core issues for your joint retirement plan.

- Next, break out the core issues into four or five general subjects. Agree to have four or five hour-long meetings to discuss each subject. These meetings should be highly structured to ensure that you stay on topic. View each topic from the perspective of common interests and future satisfaction. The intimate relationship you share with each other may seem to preclude new ideas and viewpoints. But amazingly, if you brainstorm and explore the range of possibilities, you find more to talk about than just past history. This can be a very creative exercise that produces new passions in the relationship.

• Finally, shape the plan with an eye to the future.

Scheduled meetings may seem a bit ludicrous within a lengthy marriage. But all marriages have some misunderstandings and hidden undercurrents, many of which can be resolved through a process of discovery. Many spouses have only superficial knowledge about their mate's true feelings. Using this semi-structured process facilitates a dispassionate forum for the exchange of ideas with minimal emotional and relational risk. It's a complimentary way to forge an enhanced relationship in marriage that affords a more transparent framework for retirement.

Retirement is inherently a time of change—use this change to reinvent the stage and backdrop of your relationship so that it is tailored to your needs and those of your partner. This type of interactive planning will require time, commitment, patience, and tenacity to derive maximum benefits. But it is a powerful tool for transformation.

PART-TIME WORK AND UNDEREMPLOYMENT

The majority of women are still working at age sixty, and working women are more apt to transition into part-time and temporary work prior to full retirement than men. Top corporate executives, business owners, and lawyers in larger firms often have the option at the end of careers to continue a privileged or emeritus relationship with the firm. Lateral transfers or "being kicked upstairs" to titled positions with less responsibility is also fairly common. Many retirees also do consulting work in their area of expertise, and ownership business interests often lead to a buyout agreement that permits a gradual winding down and coasting into retirement. In professional fields, a physician specialist can work flexible hours as a house physician, a staff nurse can work as a temp in a nursing home, and a teacher or psychologist can work part-time as a child day care center adviser. In the building trades, a construction manager or worker might remodel homes for relatives, and architects might design homes for friends or finish up existing projects. These are just a few means of underemployment on the road to full retirement.

Gradually transitioning from full-time to part-time work has many advantages. Gradualism affords the luxury of testing the waters and moving along the learning curve of retirement while at the same time retaining many of the social and financial benefits of work. Assuming the pay and perks don't change too drastically, most employees are quite content to cut back on their workload.

Skilled senior part-timers bring remarkable value to a company. Studies show that they are generally highly motivated, productive, reliable, and contributive of social capital. American businesses are well advised to capture a greater share of this vast pool of talent.

Starting a Family Business

Many retirees come equipped with a rich blend of expertise and experience that can be refocused on a new family business. Many retirees have developed important avocations that include hobbies, crafts, and services that can be a platform to launch a family business. Still others might pursue a joint venture or limited partnership with family or friends constructed around an existing business, an innovative idea, or mutual interest.

> *I have witnessed success in a number of businesses founded after retirement, including a specialty food store, antique toy trading, refurbishing player pianos, picture framing, a travel escort service, a catering service, and a pottery craft shop.*

The very nature of a family enterprise implies a joint effort to achieve a common mission. The atmosphere should be one of teamwork, shared adversity, and solidarity of purpose. Although there is no simple or consistent formula for success, many mom-and-pop ventures become successful businesses. The success factors for a family start-up are identical to those of any small business venture. You need a business plan, adequate capital, tenacious management, and something of quality to offer in your product or service. I have witnessed success in a number of businesses founded after retirement, including a specialty food store, antique toy trading, refurbishing player pianos, picture framing, a travel escort service, a catering service, and a pottery craft shop.

One important caveat must be understood. Nothing is ever as easy as it seems, and a start-up business is no exception. The road is rarely smooth and predictable. Most businesses require a greater degree of effort and "sweat equity" than is first projected. It warrants repeating that new businesses need a business plan, capital reserves, skilled management, and a quality product or service. If these four requirements are in place, the success rate for a new business goes from 10 percent up to 50 percent.

A chance of failure still justifies the risk. A new business is your creation. It is usually a work of passion and the fulfillment of a dream. And, if it perchance becomes a source of income, it is certain to be a source of pride and a rallying point to pull the extended family together.

A chance of failure still justifies the risk.

But working as a husband-and-wife team may be complicated. A lifetime of divergent and independent work responsibilities causes most couples to share little common ground in business and management styles. Your skills may have synergies, but the perceptions rarely coincide precisely. On the positive side, most mom-and-pop businesses have a competitive advantage over other start-ups, since inherent trust, free communication, and common purpose can be taken for granted.

Case Studies: Successful Family Businesses

Sam and Susan had a major and minor, respectively, in geology in college, but both pursued totally unrelated careers. Close to retirement, the couple started talking about potential activities they could share together after they stopped working. The common interests that surfaced included travel, hiking, and jewelry. After attending a national "rock hound" (rocks and minerals collectors) trade fair at the local convention center, they decided to explore this side interest. They attended a seminar on semiprecious gemstones at a local college. Next they took two field trips to North Carolina with the local rock hound club, and their search for rubies and garnets produced a handful of rough specimens that started a mineral collection. These trips were followed by a course in lapidary and the formation of a lab in their basement equipped to facet their gemstone treasures. Sam took the colored stone correspondence course offered by the Gemological Institute of America (GIA). With these prerequisite skills and with a minimum of additional capital, the couple began to make and sell fancy silver jewelry inlaid with turquoise, coral, and freshwater pearls. Savings were used to purchase an SUV for travel in order to market their product. They now exhibit and sell merchandise at most of the major rock hound conventions across the country. Their travel enables them to conveniently visit their grown children, who live in several distant cities. After three years the jewelry business turned a profit, and the couple continues to have a passion for this people-person business.

Monte recently retired from teaching high school Spanish, music, and physical education at a private charter school. His wife, Sally, was a domestic engineer raising six children. In college she was an art history major, and in recent years, after becoming a docent, she volunteered a day a week at the art museum. The couple loved travel, and during five European trips they visited most major tourist destinations in Spain and Portugal. The couple had several friends in the travel business, one of whom raised the possibility that they had the qualifications to be tour guides. Monte and Sally did some research and concluded that it matched their mutual interests. They applied for jobs with a national tour guide agency. They were accepted as a couple, and after six months as assistants in training, they independently guided their first tour to their favorite destination, Spain. Currently, they have signed on to conduct four tours per year. This income source plus Monte's pension have maintained their living standard, and they always happily anticipate their trips to Spain.

The successful integration into an expanded family life is the heart of the transition in retirement. Be creative, collaborative, and thorough in developing the plan to ensure the richness of your family life in the second half. Seize the opportunity to make it a new beginning.

CHAPTER 9

The Family Tree

*Y*our direct family lineage—including your parents, children, and grandchildren—has a range of needs, problems, and expectations that often directly or indirectly play a role in your retirement plans. Since we are sandwiched in between these leading and following generations, family members tend to latch onto our sense of duty and gravitate to our households when they have problems. American societal values are deeply rooted in devotion to and sacrifice for the family, and our country has legions of unsung heroes who have selflessly given their lives to the home-care of an aging parent, an ill spouse, or a disabled child.

Certainly, affluence helps provide a safety net for other members of the family. With wealth comes an increased burden, since family members usually come to you first for assistance in time of need and crisis. Being able to provide this support and rescue contributes to a sense of enhanced family cohesiveness and unity. And fortunately, wealth gives you the option to outsource many of the needs of your tribe.

No one can divine the future, and predictions from a crystal ball that go beyond six months are almost exclusively incorrect. For instance, at my annual New Year's party, I ask the twenty guests to make one-year predictions using a twenty-question quiz. The general questions range from: Will the Cincinnati Reds win their division?; At year's end will the price of gold exceed 420 dollars per ounce?; and Who will be *Time* magazine's "Person of the Year"? In this savvy group the highest grade ever recorded was 40 percent. My point here is that you don't know what will happen in the future, and you're likely at an age and state of stability that means you will be the first person your family turns to in times of need.

Infirm Parents

Approximately 60 percent of the dependent elderly live with and are cared for by adult children. Often the gradual decline and glaring needs of the older generation create a set of circumstances that challenges the close collaboration and cohesiveness of the family. Who will shoulder the duty to care for the old folks who, early in life, gave so much to you and whom you dearly love? And how will this potentially influence your retirement plans?

The role reversal from a child dependent on the parents to a child who has dependent parents is a difficult leap for all of us to make.

How is the responsibility for the parents' welfare shared, and who has the authority to make the final decision if placement in assisted living and long-term care becomes necessary? When and by whom are the car keys hidden, taking away driving privileges that may represent the last vestige of independence and control for the declining parent? How do you minimize the hazards of the stove, washer, stairs, and electrical appliances when the parent is frail and failing mentally? Who will periodically visit to ensure their welfare and take them to their doctor's appointments? How will the bills get paid, and is there enough money to cover the cost of prescription medicines? Who will provide or procure cleaning and home maintenance services? When must the old homestead be sold, and how will the proceeds be distributed? Who will be the executor of the estate and have power of attorney? An array of thorny issues almost always accompanies the extreme winter of life. These are serious questions that are resolved in different ways by every family.

The role reversal from a child dependent on the parents to a child who has dependent parents is a difficult leap for all of us to make. Since childhood we have an idealized portrait of our parents as youthful, vigorous, and capable, and this afterimage remains as their physical and mental abilities wither. At family gatherings, it is always remarkable how married couples with grown children relate to their parents in a fashion that reflects a dependent relationship from the past rather than the realities of the present. The rebellion left over from the classical love/hate relationships that exists between mothers/daughters and fathers/sons seems to linger long after it is relevant. The paradigm shift from recipient of care to caregiver is saddening. For some of us, this change reinforces the realization that we are next in line to go through the process.

Children

Adult children can bring a complex array of additional considerations and obligations. Childbearing at an older age and delayed marriages cause many families to have school-aged, single, and financially dependent children when retirement approaches. Escalating and exorbitant expense for undergraduate and graduate education can strain family resources so as to preempt early retirement. A child with physical and mental disabilities or drug and alcohol addiction may impose a significant drain on both financial and emotional family resources. Sons and daughters with failed marriages, young children, and unsustainable debt often return to the sanctuary of home for relief and assistance with child care. Single-parent homes are everywhere, and this creates a legion of latchkey kids that can benefit from the additional security and guidance of caring grandparents. And working mothers need child care programs that are often difficult to find and so expensive that the child must be cared for during the day by a grandparent. Moreover, in tragic cases where children are neglected or abandoned, the grandparents often become surrogates for the biological parents.

Overwhelmingly, children are the best investment any family can make.

This section dwells on the bad and not the beautiful, the worst-case scenarios and not the best. Overwhelmingly, children are the best investment any family can make. Love that shines to and from parent and child and back again is a gift that lasts forever. But the bottom line is that the offspring can both enrich and complicate the second half of life.

Family

For most retirees, the family situation has many pluses and minuses. Throughout the journey into retirement, as with most periods in life, duty, loyalty, love, and devotion can be complicated by independence, personal interests, and retirement dreams.

Few or no families are as dysfunctional as *The Simpsons* or *The Osbournes,* but few are as conventionally functional as those depicted on *The Donna Reed Show* or *Leave it to Beaver*. As a matter of fact, some counselors consider a truly functional family a myth or fantasy. Few families escape petty jealousies and smoldering conflicts that refuse to completely disappear. Male Oedipal feelings and the rivalry between mothers and daughters are legendary. Many brothers and sisters who were close as children end up "disowning" or dissociating themselves from one another due to relatively trivial matters that could be settled by open discussion of the issues. Even though pettiness and immature behaviors may be a problem, good feelings about one's family members usually far outweigh the bad.

As alluded to before, a close-knit and caring family is a vital critical success factor for a rich retirement. Ask those unfortunate individuals with families who are scattered and no longer keep in touch, or families that have one or more children who are divorced and have lost custody of the grandchildren. Ask people who have lost a spouse prematurely, or who are alone and isolated without family members to rely upon. Close family ties are the best security blanket for almost any ailments that occur in the second half.

> *Close family ties are the best security blanket for almost any ailments that occur in the second half.*

Retirement is a time to reinvent family life. It's fruitless to not let go of earlier disappointments, to not forgive the shortcomings of your childhood, and to not tolerate and accept your siblings as they are. Continuity and succession provide perspective about the seasons of life and our place in the universe.

Grandchildren: Special Gems

Grandchildren are a very special ingredient in your retirement formula. These creatures are delightful and usually predictably warm and wonderful (until their teenage years!). If so designed, retirement can free up time to get deeply involved in nurturing and bonding with them. Since young parents are usually much busier and preoccupied than retired grandparents, "grandparent time" can be more uncluttered and focused upon the child's interests. And bonding is remarkably easy over even mundane and ordinary activities. Moreover, while you assume the role of coach and mentor to support their childhood development, you will observe that they gradually morph into true companions, friends, students, teachers, and citizens. Plus, as the ultimate responsibility for care still rests with the parents, your time investment can be as small or as large as you choose. But your undivided and dedicated attention to their needs makes you special in their eyes. Getting involved with grandchildren is a real win-win proposition and a new avenue of activity that brings profound, heartfelt, and absolute meaning.

The family is at the core of retirement planning. In setting your expectations and goals, be certain to look both up and down the ladder of generations.

CHAPTER 10

The Messengers in Children's Clothing: Carefree Fun

*F*or most young American children, childhood is a time to explore and have fun. But as we grow up, life's demands seem to have a habit of getting in the way of unstructured fun and carefree expression. And the socialization process imposes political correctness and boundaries to our basic personalities. Retirement is an excellent time to go back to some of those earlier days, strip away acquired social veneers, expose a reserve of vibrant creativity, and go back to having fun. The uninhibited, surreal kingdom of children provides a wonderful classroom setting for seniors to relearn the art of heightened feeling.

Retirement is an excellent time to strip away acquired social veneers, expose a reserve of vibrant creativity, and go back to having fun.

Such a classroom was created for me when our entire family rented a beachfront cottage for a family reunion on Hilton Head Island. Our daughter has a little girl, Caitlin, age seven, and a boy, James, age three. Our son has two boys, Richard, age five, and Grant, age four.

The two crews of grandchildren, who had not met previously, took to each other immediately. The swimming pool, beach, and

VCR tapes provided a backdrop for shared interests. In the neutral zone of a rented house, the common tensions of sharing possessions were an infrequent problem. The playgroup of children coalesced so quickly that by the second day each claimed to be the other's best friend. In the mornings the gang ran together as a pack, and their thundering footsteps made sleeping late quite impossible. The ages of the children made little difference, and the group structure had no hierarchy. The fun was amorphous and unrestrained. At the end of the holiday, after just one week together, the children were "devastated" by the need to say goodbye but delighted by the promise that further reunions were planned. There are many ways in which young children can teach adults the articles of enjoyment—here are a few lessons you should definitely try to employ in your retirement.

1. Doing What Comes Naturally

One day, the group of grandchildren built a fairly elaborate ice cream cone sandcastle close to the breaking surf at low tide. With the rising tide, their creation became imperiled. Richard decided to save the castle by building a barrier wall. He enlisted the whole group in the project. For about an hour they enthusiastically prevented the inevitable by working together with a single purpose. In that brief time, more than a dozen creative ideas were exchanged, and the leadership role shifted frequently. Several sunbathers passing by became coaches to their efforts. Everyone was absorbed in this joyous exercise of futility replete with predictions about the next wave, comments on close calls, rebuilding damaged ramparts, and discussion about when to call it quits. It was a carefree immersion into pleasures that carry no price tag, plus a team effort that was wonderful to see and be a part of. The eventual demise of the castle was immaterial.

Spontaneity and curiosity are at the heart of our intellect, yet these gifts are often sacrificed to the requirements of conformity.

Spontaneity and curiosity are at the heart of our intellect, yet these gifts are often sacrificed to the requirements of conformity. How often do we find that spontaneity brings the most enjoyment? Retirement is a time to do what comes naturally—uninhibited, freestyle play.

2. Rules Are Made to be Broken

One morning, we took the three older children to play miniature golf. They had never played with real golf clubs but had enthusiastically prepared the night before by putting tennis balls with flimsy plastic clubs in the living room. The adults had thoroughly reviewed the issues of golf etiquette before arriving at the miniature golf course. We covered the routine of alternating turns, waiting while the other player took his turn, playing just one ball, and not taking a mulligan if you hit a bad shot. These instructions didn't last even through the first hole. Each of the children created individual rules for the game. The resulting breakdown in discipline caused the scorekeeper to discard the scorecard after just one hole. By necessity, the adults played a parallel putt-putt game and focused on making sure the party was not holding up the players behind. The kids were oblivious to performance measures except in the event of a hole-in-one or when the ball was hit out of the playing area.

The exhilaration of creative anarchy is often at odds with structure.

Despite the unorthodox nature of the game, the children had a wonderful time, and while enjoying ice cream bars afterward they made it clear that they would like to return for another round that evening and the next day. The lesson here is that the exhilaration of creative anarchy is often at odds with structure. Retirement gives a greater license to ignore structure, invent the playing field, discard performance measures, and play.

3. There Is a Season

My son and I are tennis enthusiasts. Like most suburbanites we aspire to give our kids a head-start advantage in the athletic arena. Our holiday seemed an ideal time to get the seven-year-old girl and five-year-old boy started with tennis. Both children had watched their dads play tennis and viewed professional matches on TV. After court times were reserved, the crew headed to the courts with the children, who were wearing proper white tennis attire, carrying a basket filled with twenty-five practice balls, and practicing willy-nilly swings with brand-new junior-sized racquets.

First, the various strokes and basic rules of the game were reviewed. To begin, balls were slowly hand-tossed at close range to each youngster's forehand and backhand on both sides of the court.

When any contact with the ball was made, we encouraged them and gave enthusiastic high fives if the return landed within the lines on the other side of the court. This exercise gave results that did not measure up to the grown-ups' expectations. It was a very hot, muggy summer day, and drink breaks were frequent. The children discovered that the plastic-ball canisters made excellent drinking vessels as well as weapons to instigate a water fight. This seemed like reasonable kid's play until the instructors became the targets of these young accomplices. With some difficulty the children were disarmed.

After approximately twenty minutes, we ended the formal lesson and suggested that the two pick up the tennis balls and return them to the basket. But this simple request gave rise to further creative sport that might be called tennis racquet golf or soccer tennis.

Finally, desperate to stimulate an interest in tennis, the two adults practiced while they demonstrated the "how-to" of tennis. Despite these efforts, Caitlin and Richard showed little interest and assisted by rolling balls across the court and complaining that they wanted to go home. Role modeling, infinite patience, and reasoning had a limited effect.

Learn activities at whatever pace you are comfortable with, and have patience in all things.

The time to teach and mentor grandchildren, nieces, and nephews is one of the bonuses of retirement. But if you rush the process too early, it may not produce positive results, and it usually frustrates both student and teacher. Children mature in a predictable sequence and must have a platform of basic skills to take on more complex activities. And children are very adept at letting you know when they are ready. This part of children's nature can teach you two important things: Learn activities at whatever pace you are comfortable with, and have patience in all things.

Give Back to the Youth

The beaches of South Carolina and Georgia are noted for their sand dollars. When bleached, dried, and colored, they make nifty Christmas tree ornaments and even pendants. Because the sand dollar skeleton is brittle and delicate, the better specimens do not wash up on the beach like harder seashells but are found in shallow water on the sandy bottom. The sand dollar feels spiny, hard, and moveable. Caitlin's mother had exceptional skills at harvesting sand dollars with her feet. She coached Caitlin, who quickly mastered the technique. In one afternoon, Caitlin gathered a fine collection with numerous large and small specimens to take home to her friends.

Our praise for this simple accomplishment gave Caitlin intense self-satisfaction. Retirees have the ability—even the responsibility—to be mentors and purveyors of self-esteem for our young people.

Retirees have the ability—even the responsibility—to be mentors and purveyors of self-esteem for our young people.

4. Everyone Gets Tired

The children's response to fatigue and bedtime did not change during the vacation. The long hours of travel, the bright sun and sand, the schedule of new activities, and the lighter sleep filled with anticipation all conspired to make the kids overly tired, irrationally fussy, and hyperactive at times. To make matter worse, because they were on vacation and out of their routine, they naturally resisted going to bed. Often, after presumably being asleep, they reappeared in their parents' bedroom for another bedtime story and tuck into bed. This type of behavior was expected of a child. It was not even noteworthy.

Have thicker skin and make up quickly—like a child would.

As adults, our cycles of behavior are very similar to those of school-aged children. Although better disguised, we're all victims of exhaustion and irritability that cause mood swings and impulsive actions. Sleep deficit syndrome (SDS) and sleep deprivation are commonplace in our rapid-pace society. Usually these disorders are studied as they relate to traffic accidents and on-the-job injuries. But too many relationships are also damaged by momentary lapses of reasonable behavior due to acute and chronic fatigue. Have thicker skin and make up quickly—like a child would. You can't hold grudges against someone because they acted out of turn when they were tired; we all get tired and grumpy sometimes.

5. Back to School

The summer has passed, the beach and pool have been closed for the season, the busy schedule of work, school and other commitments has been reestablished, and the vacation is just a fading dream of happiness. In I Corinthians, Chapter 13, Verse 11, it says, "When I was a child I spake as a child, I understood as a child, I thought as a child: But when I became a man, I put away childish things." Some might argue that our culture has taken this literally. Society has crafted a frame of efficiency, productivity, and politics within our lives. Many adults are conditioned to think of childish things as mindless, frivolous, pointless, and only suitable for a play fantasy world that's inappropriate to indulge in after a certain age.

Being an adult does not at all exclude the right and need for fun and unadulterated enjoyment.

Children are born with a divine gift of an unspoiled and vast intellect to capture joy and excitement. Although it may be buried, this reserve survives in all of us. Retirement is an opportunity to tap into it again and realize that being an adult does not at all exclude the right and need for fun and unadulterated enjoyment.

CHAPTER 11

Recounting the Tale

*R*etirement is a perfect time to reflect on the past and create a family history for all to enjoy. Doting on the past is not to live in the past. Revisiting the past through the kaleidoscope of retirement often gives new insights as to where we have been, where we might have gone, and where we wish to go. Since history holds no surprises, you can—with relative emotional impunity—recall the excitement, realities, and flavor of the times in which you lived through the lenses of nostalgia and reverie.

Retirement is a perfect time to reflect on the past and create a family history for all to enjoy.

When you get a chance to put some distance between yourself and the arguments and frustrations of everyday life, looking back you're always struck by how much emotional energy was wasted on fleeting concerns that now seem of little importance. Transient worries about job, marriage, children, and money were the real or imaginary threats that have long since become irrelevant. From the perch of retirement, you can more clearly see the things that have been important to you throughout your life, and those are the things you'll want to write about.

Our fast-paced society is addicted to marketing to the future. Little time is spent ruminating on ancestral relationships. Geographic mobility and the demise of the extended family have weakened family cohesiveness and the continuity of family traditions and customs. However, within most of us resides a sincere wish to occasionally turn back the clock and savor the past—in general, happiness in the present tense correlates with richness in the past.

Cleaning out and organizing the long-forgotten items that reside in the nooks and crannies of a home is a standard activity in retirement and is a good and easy start to thinking about your family history. When you look around a home, each painting, piece of furniture, knickknack, book, and spread has a history and personal pedigree. And rummaging through old artifacts such as the rusted tricycle and worn teddy bear from childhood causes fond memories to surface. Try starting your family history by going through your attic to see what old family stories are called to mind.

The Information Gap

When reflecting upon the lives of my grandparents, the last of whom died when I was in high school, I am struck by how little I know about their lives. I spent plenty of time playing with them as a child, but by then they were well beyond the prime of life, and I was too young to think of asking about their lives. My mother and father rarely discussed their childhoods in detail, and when they talked about their parents, they talked in generalities and did not drill down on their individual personality traits, their married lives together, and their accomplishments in life. Although our parents consistently characterized our grandparents as God-fearing, hard-working, considerate, and righteous immigrants, we received few details about their lives. And even these scant details will be lost to our grandchildren.

In reality, the scribbling on old, fading family photos and inscriptions in the family bibles are the only written commentary about the lives of my grandparents. It is disconcerting that it took just two generations to erase any testimony that they lived. And I think this is fairly typical of most families. Write everything down that you can remember, starting *now*— you will lose more treasured family lore than you would have thought possible by waiting.

NEW DIMENSIONS

Photography and information technology have given us a fantastic array of tools with which to record present events and document the past. These electronic devices are user-friendly, and their robust functionality makes producing a chronicle of your life and the lives of family members a relatively easy task. In effect, it nullifies any valid excuse not to leave a thorough, accessible story about your journey through life for your successors to appreciate. Retirement is the optimal time to pull together your recollections and mementos and save a picture of your life. The following are some ideas to achieve this goal.

1. Audio-Visual Methods

- Gather and sort your still photos. Date them, line them up chronologically, and then add them to a new photo album to create a visual timeline. Make sure you use a photo album that will preserve your photos, with acid-free paper and archival quality. Make brief comments in the margins to put names on the faces and identities on the events. Use your full team of family members to assist with the project. Store the duplicates and any photos that are of poor quality or little interest separately. Make tough decisions, and trim the total collection to twenty albums or less. Craft a special photo album or scrapbook for each of your children or grandchildren. It is certain to become a true keepsake.

- Dust off your 8 and 16mm movies of the family from the mid-century, and have the best ones copied by a professional to DVD. If possible, edit and condense the footage to produce a one- to two-hour show capable of holding everyone's attention, even if it is shown on an annual basis at Christmas time. Give a copy to each branch of the family.

- Gather and sort your analog and digital videos of world travel, family vacations, and the children growing up. Convert the analog to digital, and then edit and condense the footage to produce a one- to two-hour show.

- Sort and organize your many boxes of old 35mm slides. As you did with the photos, store duplicates and those that are of poor quality or uninteresting separately. Ask other family members to contribute their best slides, and develop a special collection.

Then, using modern digital equipment (camcorder, scanner, and audio-video software), make a videotape slide show with titles, commentary, and possibly music. Make a copy for each branch of the family. With any of these collections (photos, movies, videotapes, slides), be prepared to convert the "show" to the newest technology each time it changes to make them available for many generations to come.

- For your personal pleasure, take your old 78, 45, and 33 rpm records, and copy those onto audiotape. Even older record turntables and tape players have outlets that make this a simple task. The taped recordings can then be converted to a digital format for permanent storage. If you have a stereo tuner and a digital recording device, you'll even be able to convert your records directly to CD.

2. Collections

- Rummage through and sort your various old artifacts: Postcards, pennants, beer cans, dolls, stuffed animals, stamps, coins, shells, toy soldiers, trading cards, posters, and miscellaneous toys. Using library and online resources, try to arrive at a monetary valuation for any item that looks as if it might be worth something. If you have seen a similar item on the public TV program *Antiques Road Show,* obtain a professional appraisal. After cleaning and refurbishing, document which heir will receive what item.

- Take inventory of important collections such as Indian jewelry, model trains, bottles, dolls, porcelains, rare coins, stamps, and artwork. Craft a plan for distribution or sale. Does the collection belong in a museum? Will your children and grandchildren be interested in maintaining and adding to the collection? What are the avenues of selling the collection at a fair market value?

- Many homes and attics contain family heirlooms that have passed down through many generations and have appreciated in value. Get an expert opinion as to their value.

3. The Family History

- Write the family story. Consider it a chronicle of all the times in which you lived. Provide a warm snapshot of family life and the character and strengths of family members. Portray how the family circumstances and culture changed with time. Sprinkle it with your beliefs, anecdotes about events that have shaped your life, and explanations about the choices you made. Solicit additional insights from family members. In general, this family story should be a very positive commentary for subsequent generations. If you candidly uncover the family skeletons and carry on about the betrayals of life, the family network will react with indignation and disgust. We all want to be proud of our ancestry, and you will produce a prized piece of memorabilia if you write a sensitive family narrative that accentuates the richness of your heritage.

- Encourage your children and grandchildren to start personal diaries early in life. Later, these will be keepsakes that afford a wonderful view into their childhood. At a minimum, have the children keep journals describing family vacations and special occasions. Impromptu journals always capture the flavor and shared adversity of the moment as well as provide a keyhole view into a child's heart. A "family scribe" often produces a classic and priceless family archive.

- It is good medical advice to carefully document your comprehensive medical history and carry this information with you at all times (medical bracelet, computer disc, smart card, hard copy, handwritten—any medium in which it's easily and immediately accessible) in case you need emergency medical treatment. Moreover, your descendents should have more than a trivial interest in your lifetime of afflictions since, as medical science expands, it becomes increasingly apparent that many genetic factors directly link and predispose us to certain diseases. Taking it one step further, have a DNA analysis performed, or store a blood or tissue sample for later study.

Creating a written picture of your family, family life, and what the "olden times" were like to share with later generations is a fun project. Use your best storytelling abilities to recreate what it was like living into the third millennium. The changes of the past fifty years have been stunning, and yet the bigger explosion in technological and societal change is probably yet to come. Your great-great-grandchildren will likely eagerly reflect on how difficult it must have been to live in the early twenty-first century before the hydrogen-burning car, supersonic suborbital travel, conservative eugenics, and nanotechnology. It will further shock your descendents if you add the fact that part of your life was spent without television or computers, and before jet travel and the atomic age.

CHAPTER 12

The Skinny on Estate Planning

By Lewis Gatch, Attorney-at-Law

*T*his subject could be a book unto itself. Estate planning can be complicated. The purpose of this chapter is to hit the highlights and motivate you to overcome the P-word—*procrastination.* An average person works 88,000 hours before retirement yet cannot come to grips with spending 8.8 hours (the time it takes to have two meetings with a lawyer to complete a plan) on a subject that involves facing one's mortality. Get over it! We're all going to die! Do your planning now!

An average person works 88,000 hours before retirement yet cannot come to grips with spending 8.8 hours (the time it takes to have two meetings with a lawyer to complete a plan) on a subject that involves facing one's mortality.

We need to do estate planning for two reasons. First, we are living longer and need to have our assets protected (without a court guardianship) if we become disabled and can't take care of our business. Second, our real estate and retirement accounts have increased in value, and when we die, we don't want those assets subject to probate or the confiscatory federal estate tax. A plain vanilla strategy—the revocable funded living trust—can solve both those problems and many more.

HOW TO PLAN

Here are the rules of engagement. First, you must have an attorney prepare your plan. Despite their claims, financial institutions, CPAs, and insurance companies can't do estate planning. It is the practice of law performed by someone who specializes in the area—and believes it is a great idea to spare your family the expense, publicity, and frustrating delay of probate. Probate is the legal process of settling the estate of a deceased person, resolving all claims to property and money, and distributing the decedent's property—and it can take months or years to finish. A lawyer can help you avoid it.

The cost of a plan should range from $1,500 to $3,000. An experienced estate-planning attorney will tell you the fixed cost of the plan before you commission the work. The plan should include a "pour over" will, a power of attorney, and a living will.

An estate plan is just a fancy name for the way you transfer ownership of your assets to your heirs when you die.

Second, you should lead the process. The more work you do, the less legal time and expense you will incur. At your first meeting with the attorney, provide a list of your assets by account numbers, current values, and ownership; your latest financial statements; last year's income tax return, copies of all deeds, and the latest tax bills; and copies of beneficiary designations (BD) for any life insurance, annuities, or tax-deferred plans such as IRAs—not a computer printout, but a copy of the BD with *your signature*. Financial institutions frequently lose the originals. If you have any doubt about your BDs, do them again. There is no cost to obtain new BD forms or to register them with the institution. And this time, keep a copy of the signed BD among your important papers. A BD is just as important as a will or a trust because it transfers ownership of an account at your death. Often, our retirement accounts constitute most of our net worth.

An estate plan is just a fancy name for the way you transfer ownership of your assets to your heirs when you die. There are five ways to transfer assets:

1. Intestacy (*assets in decedent's name only, no will*)

2. Will (*assets in decedent's name only*)

3. Joint/Survivor Ownership (*decedent and one or more other names on an asset*)

4. Beneficiary Designation (*controls distribution of insurance and annuity proceeds, retirement accounts, pay on death [POD], or transfer on death [TOD] accounts*)

5. Living Trust

Don't use numbers one or two, because they both require probate. Use number three with caution. Even though joint and survivor ownership does avoid probate, it can cause problems. At the death of the first spouse, ownership of any jointly held asset passes to the surviving spouse, estate-tax free as a marital deduction, not using the decedent's exemption. This can trigger an avoidable estate tax at the death of the surviving spouse. Although the assets avoided probate at the first death, they will be subject to probate at the survivor's death. The survivor should not attempt to avoid probate at her death by putting children's names on assets. Any joint owner is entitled to 100 percent of the asset. Therefore, if a child has a creditor or gets divorced, the parent's assets can be taken by the creditor or ex-in-laws. Also, most people want to leave assets equally to their children, which is hard to do with the joint ownership system.

Without doubt, the best plan is the combination of beneficiary designations and the living trust to avoid probate completely and take advantage of each spouse's exemption from federal estate tax.

Avoiding Probate and Establishing a Living Trust

Why avoid probate? First of all, it is *expensive.* Attorney and executor fees often reach 6 percent of the value of your assets. It is also *public.* After it has been through the courts, anyone can obtain a copy of your will and an inventory of your assets—private information you would never have revealed during your lifetime. Probate is a *lengthy* process during which time your beneficiaries are frustrated because they do not control the assets in the probate estate. Finally, if you have any interest in real estate in any county other than the one in which you die, a duplicate probate process will be necessary in the probate court of that county and state to clear the title to the real estate interest—a process called "ancillary administration." You'll need an executor and lawyer in each location.

The goal of every adult, regardless of the value of his or her assets, should be to avoid probate. To bypass probate, establish a "living" trust, so named because you not only establish it now but re-title ownership of your assets into the name of your trust now. The trust is revocable, so you have not tied your hands if you change your mind as to beneficiaries or percentages. It is a separate entity with a life of its own (like a corporation), so when you die, it is not necessary for an executor to go to court to be appointed as the person to transfer your assets to the people named in your will. You have already designated the person who will do such a transfer, namely the successor trustee. (While you're alive and able, you are your own trustee.)

A living trust is a legal document that, just like a will, tells what you want to happen to your assets when you die—but unlike a will, it prevents the court from controlling your assets if you become incapacitated.

Your trust is the substitute for the will—a far superior substitute. What is a living trust? It is a legal document (contract) that, just like a will, dictates what you want to happen to your assets when you die. But unlike a will, it prevents the court from controlling your assets if you become incapacitated. After you set up a living trust, you transfer ownership of assets to that trust, such as from "John Rogers and Mary Rogers, husband and wife," to "John Rogers and Mary Rogers, Trustees under trust dated November 15, 2009." Legally, you no longer own anything, so there is nothing for the courts to control when you die or become incapacitated. Your trust, which you control, owns the assets. The concept is simple, but it keeps you and your family out of the courts.

You do not lose control of your assets at any point in this process. As trustee of your trust, you can do anything you could do before. You can buy, sell, borrow against your assets, change, or even cancel your trust. Remember, it is revocable. You even file the same income tax returns with your Social Security number. Nothing changes but the names on the titles. It is not hard to transfer assets into your trust. Your attorney, financial adviser, and insurance agent can help. The attorney should prepare and record the new deeds. Your living trust will also own all your personal property such as jewelry, art, and antiques, even though those assets do not have titles. Your attorney will have you put your personal property into the trust without itemizing it. (See Chapter 19 for suggestions about distribution of personal property.) You should change beneficiary designations on your insurance and annuities to take advantage of tax planning, so the court cannot control any property if a beneficiary is incapacitated or no longer living when you die.

Establishing a living trust does take some time, but you can and should take that time now—or your family will be paying courts and attorneys to do it later. The living trust is a wonderful organizational tool because all your assets are brought together under one plan. Once you have done a trust, do not delay "funding" it. Your car will not work unless you put gas in it. Your trust will not work unless you put your assets into it.

Power of Attorney

We are living longer than we used to, and a long life increases the chance of incapacitation. If you cannot take care of property and pay your bills due to mental or physical incapacity such as heart attack, stroke, or Alzheimer's, you may well be subjected to a court monitor to make your decisions for you. Once a court takes control, until you recover or die, the court—not your family—dictates how your assets are used to care for you. This process can be embarrassing, time consuming, expensive, and difficult to end if you recover. What's more, it does not replace probate at death. Your family could have to go through the court system *twice.*

> *Once a court takes control, until you recover or die, the court—not your family—dictates how your assets are used to care for you.*

A durable power of attorney lets you name someone to manage your financial affairs if you cannot. An immediate power of attorney can be used even if you are competent. The immediate power should be used with great caution—many financial institutions will not honor a power of attorney unless it is on their form. And sometimes a power of attorney may work *too* well, giving your agent a blank check to do whatever he wants with your assets. The living trust provides better control and accountability when a successor trustee or a co-trustee manages your affairs while you are incapacitated. Powers of attorney are not well understood. The agent need not be an attorney-at-law. Any adult can be so designated. They are known as "attorney-in-fact." The power of attorney dies when you die. It cannot be used to pay the funeral bill, final income tax, or any other expenses.

Avoiding the Federal Estate Tax

A common mistake made by many higher net-worth families is to leave everything to the surviving spouse by will or have all assets held jointly. Why is this a mistake? Because when the first spouse dies (usually the husband, in the United States), his exemption from federal estate tax is wasted. When the wife thereafter dies, only her exemption is available. If the assets exceed $3.5 million, then the tax levied at the rate of 37 percent quickly brackets up to 45 percent and is levied on the excess over the amount of the survivor's exemption. The husband's exemption is lost forever.

For a husband and wife who will have assets in excess of the estate tax exemption at the death of the survivor, their second goal (after avoiding probate) should be to avoid federal estate tax. Under current law, each person has an exemption of $3.5 million as of January 1, 2009. The tax is scheduled to be repealed in 2010, only to be reinstated with an exemption of $1 million in 2011. If your assets will exceed $3.5 million, it's crucial that you do your tax planning now. The tax is levied on everything you own including financial assets, life insurance, retirement benefits, real estate, and personal property. You don't want your heirs to pay a tax that could have been avoided.

The simple way to finesse the tax is for each spouse to have a living trust, and to have each trust own or be the beneficiary of roughly half of the family assets. Then, when the husband dies, his exemption will be used to shelter the assets in his trust from estate tax. The wife, as the trustee of the husband's trust, will control the trust and manage the investments. She will be entitled to income and principal from the trust. She will have economic use of the trust similar to ownership, but since the assets stay in the husband's trust during her lifetime, they will not be taxed at her death. Thus the name "bypass" trust, as mentioned earlier. The assets in the trust of the first to die bypass tax at the second death. By the use of each exemption, $7 million can be passed to the children free of tax, leaving Uncle Sam out as a beneficiary of $1,575,000 ($3,500,000 at 45 percent tax).

Albert Einstein said tax-free compounding is the eighth wonder of the world.

Keeping in mind the uncertainty about what the exemption might be at your death, your attorney should include a flexible provision in your trust that allows it to be tax efficient regardless of the amount of the federal estate tax exemption when you die.

Tax-Deferred Assets (Retirement Accounts)

Retirement accounts such as IRAs and 401(k)s present a special planning problem, especially when children are the beneficiaries. These accounts can be subject to an estate tax of up to 45 percent and an income tax of up to 35 percent, leaving the children a mere 30 cents on the dollar after taxes. If your plan includes gifts to a charity, you should do such gifting by making the charity the beneficiary of your IRA, or a portion of it. Leave other assets to your children. The charity will receive the IRA tax-free compared to the possible 70 percent tax burden to your children.

If you do make children the beneficiary of your IRA, vehemently tell them now that they should take advantage of the new "stretch-out" rule, which allows them to defer income tax on most of the IRA throughout their lifetime. (Albert Einstein said tax-free compounding is the eighth wonder of the world.) For example, assume at your death that your forty-eight-year-old child inherits your $360,000 IRA. Your child has a life expectancy under the IRS table of thirty-six years, thus requiring your child to withdraw $10,000 in the first year. Further assume that the account earned 8 percent, or $28,800. After the first-year withdrawal of $10,000 (on which the child would pay income tax), the account would have grown to $378,800. By the time the child retires, he or she will have thus built up a substantial retirement account, even after taking the required minimum distribution each year, which is determined by age.

Annual Exclusion Gifts

The same tax that applies to monetary or property transfers at death applies to transfers during life, except it is then called the "gift" tax. The exemption from this tax is $1 million. Nevertheless, you can make gifts up to $12,000 per person per year without eating into the $1 million exemption. These are called *annual exclusion* gifts. Higher net-worth families use these to great advantage to transfer assets to the next generation over a period of years. If the annual gifts are kept within the exclusion amount, no gift tax return must be filed. In addition to the annual exclusion amount, you can pay family members' medical expenses and school tuition in unlimited amounts. Any such payments must be made directly to the medical care provider or the school.

AN ESTATE-PLANNING CASE STUDY

Here's a true situation that illustrates the flexibility and creativity of trust planning. A mother with a son and a grandson has a portfolio of $800,000. Even though her son is forty-five, he is still "finding himself"—meaning he is not gainfully employed, a playboy. Wanting to provide her grandson a college education and to protect her assets from her son's lifestyle, the mother has established a trust of which she is the trustee, with a local bank as the successor trustee. The trust provides that after her death the corporate trustee will make sure the grandson is educated and will distribute income to the son equal to his W-2 (or Schedule C if he is self-employed). Feeling that the son will mature eventually, the mother's trust states that if the son produces a W-2 of $30,000 a year or more for ten years in a row, he captures half of the principal of the trust outright.

This is called an "incentive" trust. It makes the point that, unlike a will, a trust does not have to die with you. Your assets can continue in trust, managed by the person or corporate trustee you have chosen, until your beneficiaries reach the age and capacity when they should inherit. By adding a different set of controls, assets can be maintained in the family bloodline for generations even though a child divorces or dies. Long life trusts are particularly valuable for assets that should be held in indivisible form, such as a vacation cottage, a closely held business, a farm, or investment real estate.

Some people tell their children what assets they own and how they will be distributed; others do not. There is no right or wrong answer. At a minimum, however, you should notify the children who will be in charge of your affairs where your records are kept, in the event of your incapacity or death. If you have a safe at home, tell the children the combination or where the key is kept. If you have a safe deposit box, give a third person access to the box so that at your death or disability, a court order will not be necessary to enter the box. In most states, the bank no longer seals the box when someone dies—so the old "race to the bank before the funeral" is no longer run.

If you use a revocable, funded living trust, you will have created a well-organized paper trail during the funding process. Keep your records in one place, and update them at least once a year. Include funeral instructions, people to be notified in the event of your death, and a family tree that tells the cause of death of your ancestors—information that could be valuable to your grandchildren.

SECTION IV:

Safeguard Your Retirement Money

★

★ CHAPTER 13 ★

Personal Finances:
A Realistic Approach

etirement is usually accompanied by a major reallocation and juggling of assets. Pensions, profit sharing, and 401(k) plans are rolled over into IRAs with new plan administrators and advisers. Annuities, life and health insurance coverage, and company severance packages are reviewed. Wills and trusts are updated to reflect new circumstances and legacy plans. Medicare and Social Security benefits begin to kick in. The expected decline in current income and earning power prompts critical assessment of spending habits, budgets, investment performance, and "what if" scenarios. Remember: You most likely always want to consult an expert during this phase of evaluation and planning.

THE HOMESTEAD

The worth of your home and where it will go when you're gone is often a prime concern at retirement—the equity in your house often represents the majority of your assets. However, these assets do not generate income to supplement your fixed income but add to your expenses through maintenance and property taxes.

By retirement, most homeowners have paid off their home mortgages. With an excessive amount of your wealth tied up in home equity, you'll naturally want to consider ways to convert some of that equity into productive investments and cash. Banks and other lenders offer home equity and home improvement loans to partially achieve this conversion. And in recent years, reverse mortgages have become a creative way to convert all or most of your home equity into a type of annuity. In a reverse mortgage, the home is purchased by a financial institution, and in return, the previous homeowner is paid a monthly fixed or variable amount of the principal and interest over a specified period of years.

The decision to sell your home is often the most agonizing and stressful one you will ever be called upon to make.

Many retirees sell their larger residences and move to smaller quarters or rented apartments upon retirement, and some couples consider a move to a development that offers variable living options such as independent living, assisted living, and nursing-home care. The decision to sell your home is often the most agonizing and stressful one you will ever be called upon to make. Most homes become an extension of the families' identity—who wants to give up their home after it took so many years to understand the home's idiosyncrasies, systems, and noises?

In selling the home, myriad factors must be considered: What are the financial factors that influence the decision-making process? What medical problems or physical limitations might need to be factored in? Where do your children live, and how dependent upon you are they? How encouraging and supportive is your spouse about a move? How determined are you to stay in your present home? Finally, you need to assess how a move will change the social life and routine that you have established over many years.

All relocation choices have pros and cons. The most compelling pro is that it can convert a nonproductive asset into a productive one that can supplement your fixed income. Moreover, smaller quarters, especially if they have no steps to climb and are of more recent construction, are less demanding on the body and less costly to maintain. And most dedicated retirement communities offer a broad range of planned group activities that quickly establish new social relationships. Finally, a new location is frequently chosen to bring you closer to other family members and friends.

There are cons to relocating, as well. You may feel you are sacrificing an identity you have with a home and the potential loss of a circle of friends close by in the neighborhood. Plus having to sort through, dispose of, and part with furniture and furnishings that have become familiar friends in order to fit into smaller quarters is always an unpleasant and emotionally draining task. Regardless of the reasons for moving, accept the fact that a move is always stressful and disorienting. With time, and in most instances, you will find that a well-planned, smart move will improve the quality of your life and the lives of those around you.

THE SAVINGS RATE

In the early part of the twentieth century, before Social Security and retirement plans, American culture was more grounded in the puritan ethic of self-sufficiency and thrift. Earlier generations, especially those who lived through the Great Depression of the 1930s, lived by mottoes such as "Save for a rainy day," "Money doesn't grow on trees," and "Children must appreciate the value of a dollar." During those times, retirement as we know it today was a nebulous dream beyond the reach of ordinary people—and when it did happen, retirement was an intruder that reared its ugly head due to debility, serious illness, or death.

Today, things are much different. Post–World War II's stable, growing economy led the way for the "credit generation," and the self-denial and shared adversity of the Depression era was pushed aside by easy living on borrowed money. The mores of disciplined saving and sacrifice have gradually faded into a new fabric of exuberant materialism, high expectations, and instant gratification. As a byproduct of this abundance, retirement has ceased to be a privilege for just a small cohort of wealthy individuals and has populated the desires and expectations of virtually all workers.

Since World War II, the savings rate of American families has declined dramatically. Consumers are constantly bombarded and beguiled by advertising. Trying to maintain a fashionable lifestyle and an overachieving standard of living can become irresistible; Americans tend to spend more than they earn, and most live from paycheck to paycheck or "hand to mouth." Consequently, a high percentage of families are burdened with excessive debt and are doing a balancing act just to meet the monthly payments on credit-card balances, home mortgages, insurance policies, and car payments. People seek the advice of debt counselors to consolidate loan payments and put forth a disciplined plan to escape from the encumbrances of debt. When all else fails, personal bankruptcy protection often becomes necessary. The rate of bankruptcy in America is phenomenally high.

Since World War II, the savings rate of American families has declined dramatically.

The national savings rate in America, including both the private and public sector, is miniscule when compared to other developed nations. Most wealth in America is created on paper through the increase in real-estate values and rising stock-market prices. Historically, the savings rate on personal earned income averaged 1.5–2.5 percent, but in some recent quarters the savings rate has been negative. And this is in a society where the average family has two wage earners in order to make ends meet.

RETIREMENT ASSETS

Social Security payments are the primary safety net for retirees. However, according to recent studies, 401(k)plans and other defined-contribution plans have a growing role in retirement, and by the year 2025 the amount of wealth accrued in 401(k) plans will equal that in Social Security benefits. But the participation rate and composition of 401(k)plans is troubling. As of 2005, 26 percent of eligible workers failed to join 401(k) plans and less than 10 percent contributed the maximum amount allowed. In many of these plans, the majority of contributions are invested primarily in the shares of the parent company. This creates a serious problem if the company shares decline in value or if the company fails.

Additionally, 25 percent of workers who change jobs do not reinvest the cash from their 401(k) in another qualified plan at their new employer.

Today there are over 63 million people with defined-contribution plans. This type of plan has advantages for both the employee and employer. The employees can easily roll over or cash out the accrued benefits when they move to a new job. And a defined-contribution plan places fewer rigid funding requirements on the employer when compared to a traditional pension plan.

The majority of soon-to-be-retired Americans acknowledge that they should have started saving earlier in their careers.

Despite the transitioning of employers to defined-contribution plans, there remain a large number of Americans with old-fashioned pension plans that promise a set schedule of continuing payments in retirement. The total pension liability for the thirty thousand companies who still offer these plans is estimated to exceed $1 trillion, and many of these plans are markedly underfunded. If a company becomes insolvent, the insurer of last resort is the Pension Benefit Guaranty Corp. (PBGC), a government agency that was created to bail out bankrupt pension plans. But there is a cap: If a retiree's pension benefit is above a specified amount, the PBGC will reduce the benefit and the retiree's maximum payment.

Overall, most retirees have insufficient aggregate wealth to maintain the same standard of living that they enjoyed while working.

It is no surprise that the majority of soon-to-be-retired Americans acknowledge that they should have started saving earlier in their careers and been more conscientious about tucking away a higher percentage of their earnings.

A standard question arises again and again: When is the best time to start saving for retirement? The stock answer is an unequivocal "now," and it should be prefaced by *"it is never too late."* It is wise to start making contributions to your retirement when you receive that first paycheck. But even if only five or ten years remain until retirement, there are ways to accelerate your rate of saving to fund an increasing portion of retirement needs. For laggards the tax codes have liberalized the amounts of income that can be placed tax-free in tax-deferred retirement accounts.

> *When is the best time to start saving for retirement? The stock answer is an unequivocal "now," and it should be prefaced by "it is never too late."*

Starting early provides a longer time frame for retirement accounts to grow through compounding interest and dividends, as well as appreciation in stocks, bonds, real estate, and tangibles. The greater the number of years invested, the greater the probability that a small investment will become a sizable asset. This is called financial leverage. To give an example, consider that over the past forty years, investments in the stock market have produced an annual average total return of about 12 percent. At this rate of return,

$1,000 invested at age twenty would grow to $162,629.37 at age sixty-five. Based on this assumption, an investment of just $10,000 would produce a millionaire by age sixty and ample surplus to fund your retirement whims at age sixty-five. However, be cautious with these projections—the new world economy may result in lower rates of return during the next forty years. Assuming a lower hurtle rate, you would need to save more to achieve the same result.

HOW MUCH MONEY IS ENOUGH?

How much money do you need to retire? If you ask dozens of retirees that question, you'll get dozens of different answers. Jokingly, about half offer ridiculous figures such as fifteen to twenty million. Few can come up with a valid estimate, and most concede that they do not know with certainty. It is more a guessing game than an accurate assessment.

There are too many variables with unpredictable consequences to make a precise forecast for financial needs.

In reality, the only realistic answer is "it depends." Each year in retirement has different financial requirements. With later marriages, earlier retirements, and postponed child rearing, many retirees continue to shoulder significant financial burdens for teenage children. Some retirees may wish to move to a warmer climate where real estate and living expenses are higher, or become "snowbirds" and purchase a second home in the South. Some unforeseen events can cloud the picture. There are too many variables with unpredictable consequences to make a precise forecast for financial needs.

Case Study

Marjorie and Nate just retired. They have no debts, a home appraised at $300,000, $150,000 in bank CDs, and combined IRAs worth $600,000. Their Social Security checks total $1,500 per month. They jointly crafted an exciting retirement plan that includes buying a motor home to travel four months a year, exploring national parks and visiting friends and relatives. They have carefully created a budget that calls for annual expenditures of $68,350. With about $25,000 in income from Social Security and CDs and an estimated withdrawal of only $60,000 from their IRA yearly, the $1,050,000 in their gross estate would seem adequate to cover any of their financial needs in retirement.

But, as in many retirement scenarios, threatening contingencies exist. In this particular case, a daughter is in a troubled marriage, and she and her two children may need to temporarily return home to live. A son-in-law has talked about starting a landscaping business and has hinted that he might ask for a personal loan or a partnership arrangement. Moreover, interest rates on reinvested CDs may decline, or the stock market might plunge. And serious illness or disability may befall Marjorie or Nate and consume a large share of their reserves. We must conclude that financial planning for retirement is as much an art as it is a science. It has a definite intuitive component.

New Spending Habits

Most individuals underestimate retirement living expenses, especially during the first two or three years. Indeed, retirement seems to open the floodgates for creative new ways to spend money. You purchase "toys" that support a new hobby such as photography or woodworking, and playthings such as a new pickup truck or power washer. The hardware and major discount stores become analogous to the candy store you frequented in your youth. Travel brochures become standard reading material, and you have more time to be seduced by items advertised in catalogs, on websites, and in store windows. The kitchen at home is "closed," and eating out becomes more of a routine. You tend to spend more on the grandchildren. Consequently, in the first few years it is common for retirees to run through more after-tax income than in the last year of work. The bumper sticker that boasts, *"We're spending our children's inheritance,"* contains more than just an element of truth.

> *Most individuals underestimate retirement living expenses, especially during the first two or three years.*

The Reality

The lump sum aggregate amount contained in retirement accounts, when added to Social Security benefits, often seems reassuringly adequate. However, the dollars withdrawn from a retirement account are usually before-tax dollars, and depending on your income bracket, Social Security payments are also before-tax dollars. After taking

$100,000 from your account, you must pay both federal and state taxes as if it were regular income. In a 25 percent tax bracket, this leaves you with only $75,000 of disposable income. Moreover, there are penalties if you take early withdrawals before age fifty-nine-and-a-half from your IRA, or do not take mandatory distributions after you reach age seventy. This emphasizes the need to calculate net worth and retirement accounts from an after-tax perspective.

You can bank on one thing: Government bills, notes, and bonds will be paid off at their face value at the maturity date.

Inflation must also be factored into the wealth equation. And even if your account is invested in the relatively safe haven of U.S. Treasury bonds, municipal bonds, secured mortgage futures, or high-grade corporate debt instruments, the market value of the issues and rates of return can fluctuate as widely as the Dow industrials. Just like any other type of investment, bonds carry a risk-and-reward profile. Generally their valuations move in the opposite direction from stock equities, but the same market forces impact them. You can bank on one thing: Government bills, notes, and bonds will be paid off at their face value at the maturity date.

As a general rule it is prudent for retirees to add up net wealth through conservative lenses. It is better to underestimate than to overestimate, and it is prudent to select a projected rate of return on your productive investments that uses a low hurtle rate. A long-range 5 to 7 percent return is low enough to compensate for the most adverse conditions.

OKAY, BUT HOW MUCH MONEY IS ENOUGH?

A benchmark that is frequently recommended by financial advisers is that your retirement funds should, over the long haul, be able to provide 75 percent of average pre-retirement gross income. If your average gross income while employed was $80,000, you should target $60,000. This figure assumes that you have no significant outstanding debts or liabilities. The rationale is that, with this amount of gross income, the sacrifices to your standard of living should be minimal and easily managed.

Financial planners delight in this 75 percent benchmark for a number of reasons. In the first place, it is a wake-up call, since few retirees have accumulated the financial assets to produce this level of passive income from interest, rents, dividends, and IRA appreciation without having to spend some portion of the underlying principal year after year. This realization (often spurred by the planners themselves) stimulates personal savings and an increase in the amount of money tucked away yearly in retirement plans. Financial advisers are the "white knights" ready to come to your rescue.

But 75 percent is a hefty figure. Let's do the numbers to achieve $60,000 of annual income. Social Security and miscellaneous income reasonably would provide $25,000. This would leave a difference of $35,000. If you had a conservative 5 percent return on investments, you would need $700,000 to generate that $35,000 annually without eating into the principal. But let's assume that your nest egg of productive investments is only $350,000. This would leave a $17,500 difference in the first year.

To further manipulate the numbers, let's assume this $17,500 deficit needs to be withdrawn from your retirement savings year after year. In that case, your retirement account of $350,000 would be halved between the eighth and ninth year of retirement and you would run out of money in the fourteenth year. You must also make allowances for inflation, the potential for Social Security and Medicare benefits to be cut, and changes in the tax code.

Starting to save early and often is the central imperative for giving you the surplus of wealth that can spare you this worry.

Projecting and crunching real numbers is a good learning exercise, and when used properly can provide a rough template or reference point around which to evaluate your financial position when entering retirement. Starting to save early and often is the central imperative for giving you the surplus of wealth that can spare you this worry.

Taking Stock and Making Do

We need to be realistic. Few retirees have sufficient investment income to supply ongoing cash needs without significant erosion of the principal. On average, retirees over age sixty-five derive the majority of their income from Social Security. Income from part-time work accounts for about 25 percent. This supplemental income is especially important for older single women and low-income workers with modest retirement and Social Security benefits.

In general, we can conclude that most retirements are underfunded. Most retirees have to accept a simple preservation strategy—a strategy once highly regarded: Living within your means. It is basically accepting and living within the confines of scarce resources and limiting spending to those items that bring the most value and utility.

Most retirees have to accept a simple preservation strategy—a strategy once highly regarded: Living within your means.

Budgeting limited resources requires both an understanding of costs and considerable planning. Families that adhere to a yearly budgeting process are well versed in the routine of choosing between alternatives.

Actually taking the time to meticulously put together a monthly and yearly family budget sheds light on many of the problems that confront retirees who find themselves left with a marginal fixed income. Let's outline the process. Although tedious, sorting through income and expenses is fairly straightforward and easy. Many simple computer programs help with the process by providing standardized templates or forms. First, calculate your income from the preceding year. Then track all monthly and aggregate yearly expenses using canceled checks, cash receipts, and credit card purchases. Add an estimate of small items purchased with cash. It may also be helpful to segregate expenses into standard categories, such as:

- Car expenses

- Debt payments

- Department stores

- Grocery stores

- Home maintenance and taxes

- Entertainment and dining out

- Charitable giving

- Telephone, water, and energy expense

- Travel/vacations

- Medical costs/pharmacy

- Club dues

- Books, daily papers, and magazines

- Home improvements

- Accounting and legal expenses

List every expense for each category. Then, drill down further and separate the expenses into two columns, one for absolutely essential items or nondiscretionary spending, and the other for nonessential or discretionary spending. Then comes the hard part: making cuts. Cull the nonessential or discretionary bin by eliminating those items that produce the least value. Leave some wiggle room at the cut, and hold on to your records, just in case— fate might bring a windfall from the lottery, inheritance, an astute investment, or a mineral strike on your farm.

For many, the successful adjustment to a fixed-income budgeting process holds the keys to complete financial independence in retirement. When you are faced with a scarcity of dollars, the value and the purchasing power of the dollar must increase. Within reason, almost any budget can be stretched to accommodate the essential needs placed on it.

For many, the successful adjustment to a fixed income budgeting process holds the keys to complete financial independence in retirement.

Spending on some items, such as clothing, your car, entertainment, and club memberships usually decreases in retirement. Others increase, such as travel, food, and home-repair expense. Try to estimate the impact that changes in spending patterns will produce.

Many good things are free, such as the city parks, libraries, special concerts, church functions, some museums, and so on. Take advantage of a broad array of discount cards that offer seniors a 10–15 percent discount that is often honored by airlines, hotels, restaurants, movie theaters, and a wide range of retailers. The crucial point is that you must define and understand all expenses and then make those cuts that cause the least amount of inconvenience and sacrifice. View spending as a "competitive game" to get the most value and utility for the least number of dollars. Chapter 18 outlines the art and science of buying and selling, and it provides additional strategies to make dollars stretch.

CHAPTER 14

The New Economy

*T*he stock market is an investment of profound volatili-ty—if you asked four people about the state of the econ-omy and whether it is a good time to invest in stocks and bonds, you'll get four different opinions with no consensus or even a hint of certainty about the short- or long-term performance of the stock market. The disparate insights are as far apart as the opposite poles of bullish and bearish sentiment. If you were a stock analyst you would euphemistically describe this as a "dispersion" of opinion that possibly reflects a lack of "transparency" of corporate profit projections and unsettled world markets. Of course, what it really means is that no one really knows what the stock market will do tomorrow.

Economists and market analysts take the economic pulse and make forecasts using many economic indicators. These forecasts are tightly interwoven with government's fiscal (spending) and monetary policies (interest rates and money supply). Some of the more important factors in predicting market trends include: ·

- Government budget deficits—estimated accumulated federal deficit of $9.2 trillion in 2008

- The Federal Open Market Committee (FOMC) discount rate and the ten-year Treasury bond yield—(3.5 percent and about

3.76 percent respectively in February 2008)

- The unemployment rate and new weekly unemployment claims—(4.9 percent unemployment in February 2008)

- Consumer confidence and total personal consumption—(Consumer confidence 69.6 percent in February 2008)

- Gross domestic product (GDP) and percentage change—($13 trillion with about 1.6 percent increase in 2007)

- Current account balances or international trade deficit—(deficit of $752 billion in 2007–8)

- Inflation rates as measured by the consumer (CPI) and producer price indices (PPI)—(both 4.1 percent 2007)

- Strength of the dollar against the euro, yen, and yuan (.7, 107, and 8 equal one dollar respectively in 2008)

- Consumer debt growth (consumer debt increased 7.76 percent of GDP in 2007)

- Housing starts and existing home sales—(1.01 million units and 4.89 million units in 2007 respectively; a decline of 38.2 percent and 22.01 percent respectively)

- Personal disposable income and personal savings rates—(5.81 percent increase and 0 percent in 2007 respectively)

Analysts use these indicators and various formulas to make market-trend predictions, which are then framed within the context of previous business cycles dating back to the nineteenth century. Based upon these predictions and the historical trends, the government has the authority to increase or decrease fiscal spending to help maintain a sustainable level of economic growth. The Federal Reserve Board can institute a liberal or restrictive monetary policy (money supply) designed to counter threats from inflation, recession, and stagnant economic growth.

The experts are adrift in a sea of conflicting data and lack of market transparency.

Unfortunately, the economy changes course slowly, and measures to counteract the pendulum swings may take many months or even years to kick in. Likewise, the economic indicators are imprecise gauges and can often be misleading, and there are too many variables to fit neatly into one scientific formula. While one sector of the economy seems to be performing well, others may be moving in the opposite direction. Thus, forecasts are often grossly inaccurate, and the use of a crystal ball or Ouija board often seems to give equally good results as the analysts. This fickle unpredictability explains why one analyst or mutual fund may capture the spotlight for one or maybe two years and then go into the tank. It also explains why one style of investing may be most suitable for one set of economic circumstances but not others. The experts are adrift in a sea of conflicting data and lack of market transparency.

Therefore, stockbrokers, financial advisers, and market specialists have a broad range of opinions with each generating a bullish or bearish outlook based on different data derived from the same body of information. If you watch the *Nightly Business Report* or *Wall Street Week* on TV, you quickly come to realize that the commentators often express diametrically opposite views about economic performance and the momentum and swings within the economy. The economy's globalization, with the emergence of many important overseas stock exchanges and rapidly growing foreign economies, has added to the complexity of forecasting. All of these factors have contributed to the financial community's bad case of opinion dispersion.

FUTURE TRENDS AND EXPECTATIONS

The new world order and globalization of the economy bring new forces to the financial markets. Some of these forces may profoundly influence returns on investments. Obviously, this is of great importance to the retirees who rely on investment income. Here four trends that are timely and relevant in this new era, trends that will only become more important:

- Revolutions in Information Technology

- Globalization of Markets

- Savvy Customers

- Deregulation and Privatization

1. Revolutions in Information Technology

In the late 1990s, a technological explosion of innovation and new business ventures with ballistic growth projections produced a stock market bubble. But despite significant growth rates and rapidly rising revenues, the business models of the dot-com and bio-tech firms failed to produce profits while rapidly burning through copious amounts of cash and venture capital. Consequently, the richly priced equities market imploded.

Even though the dot-com mania may no longer power the stock market, the information technology (IT) evolution and revolution is still alive and well. It has fundamentally changed the way businesses operate by providing the tools to transfer and manage information instantly. Just-in-time supply, modular-flexible-automated manufacturing, efficient consumer response, e-commerce, and disintermediation are new business terms that describe a marketplace that operates at the speed of light with direct interconnectivity and feedback loops within the entire supply and demand chain. Computer-assisted design (CAD) shortens the development cycle of new products, and computerized information-sharing facilitates the reverse engineering (duplication) of innovation so that new brands and equivalent products quickly appear. Today's off-the-shelf computer software and the free or inexpensive downloads of software programs from the Internet afford awesome capabilities without the expense of customized software programming.

Even though the dot-com mania may no longer power the stock market, the information technology (IT) evolution and revolution is still alive and well.

Electronic automation accounts for the majority of the marked increase in worker productivity in recent years, and the stagnation of job creation in recent years, may relate in part to this increase in worker productivity.

Electronic automation also lowers the costs of entry into business. It speeds the arrival of new competitors and alternate products that quickly destroy the capability of extraordinary profits. As a consequence, to compete you must be nimble and accepting of a shortened product life cycle. With such rapid compression, new innovations quickly become victim to mature market forces where price competition lowers profit margins. New products quickly evolve into commodities. As an example, who would have ever predicted that the computer would become just a "box" commodity item? With shrinking profit margins comes a decrease in return on investment.

2. Globalization of Markets

Globalization of markets and free trade has produced a vast marketplace where capital, human resources, and goods readily flow between countries. Migration and outsourcing of U.S. manufacturing to foreign countries have become well-publicized and perplexing trends in recent years. But this move to overseas production is profitable, and in all probability the expatriation of U.S. jobs will increase in the coming years due to the extremely low labor costs in the Third World and Asia. A ten-to-one ratio comparison between the high wages in the United States and the low wages in China and India is no exaggeration. If your cost of production is 50 percent lower in China, how can you continue to compete in the competitive U.S. market if you continue to manufacture here at home?

Many countries emerging as major economic players, such as China, Russia, and India, with populations running into the billions, are developing a vast reservoir of highly educated individuals. In

2003, China graduated twice the number of engineers as the United States, and India is producing a unique brand of IT industrial infrastructure that mirrors Silicon Valley. This low-pay intellectual capital is now luring the higher-paying white-collar and service jobs away from America. The United States no longer holds the patent on the "knowledge worker."

Other economic barometers also drive job migration. Environmental regulations for air and water pollution are more stringent in the United States, as are the rules for the disposal of toxic and radioactive waste. Business oversight, accounting practices, and reporting requirements are often rudimentary and lack standardization in some countries as compared to the United States. There are fewer restrictive labor laws, as well as a shelter for earnings and deferred executive compensation that deprives the IRS of tax dollars.

Globalization of markets and free trade has produced a vast marketplace where capital, human resources, and goods readily flow between countries.

The opening of foreign markets to American products is very tricky—every country has its own peculiar mix of trading practices. Unfair or asymmetrical trading practices such as tariffs, subsidies, dumping, quotas, currency manipulation, cultural barriers, permit requirements, political bribes, corruption, and geopolitical issues abound in some areas, making foreign trade a complicated and often risky prospect.

David Ricardo, a nineteenth-century English economist, was the first to give form to the arguments for free trade. Today, the doctrine of free trade has been elevated to the status of the Holy Grail, and its disciples dominate both the Republican and Democratic parties. From an economic perspective, the tenets of competitive advantage and the productivity frontier model define free trade. Production moves naturally to the country with the greatest efficiency and lowest cost structure. But today, with other things being equal, when the asymmetry of wage scales between the developed and underdeveloped world is about ten to one, competitive advantage is no longer a tenable concept to characterize a fair, level playing field. The advantage is no longer competitive but rather absolute. It will take many decades to raise the underdeveloped world to our standard of living. In the worst-case scenario, unregulated free trade may make the balance of payment deficits unsustainable, further devalue the American dollar, and continue the shifting of American manufacturing overseas.

Free trade is widely accepted as the engine of economic growth and international development. Hordes of competitors compete in the world market to drive price competition that produces lower prices for the U.S. consumer. But, what are the attendant costs to the capitalistic U.S. economy? Without pricing power, how can corporate America generate the retained earnings to make new investments in capital equipment and still pay investors a decent return on investment?

3. Savvy Customers

Customers have come to expect and demand more from the products they buy and the companies that produce them. In response, successful businesses have improved customer service, tailored their products to meet customer wants as well as needs, and aspired to create a satisfying buying experience that creates customer loyalty.

Today's consumers are well informed and extremely price conscious. They expect discounts, year-round sales, everyday low prices, and outlet-store bargains. The meteoric rise of Wal-Mart and Target attests to a pervasive discount mentality of the American shoppers, and this, in turn, explains the gradual demise of Main Street America.

> *Today's consumers are well-informed and extremely price-conscious.*

Along with staying price-conscious, the Internet and print resources give today's consumer access to detailed information about almost any product or service without even a trip to the store. Since the market is so competitive, people are more concerned about getting the best quality for the price. They are also starting to factor in greater concerns, such as which manufacturer is the most environmentally friendly. With two cars in an average household, huge suburban shopping malls, and plenty of vendors, the average American has ample opportunity to make purchases of good quality that support issues they care about, at the lowest cost. Indeed, the savvy consumer is well fortified to vote with his or her pocketbook and further shrink profit margins for American retailers and service providers.

4. Deregulation and Privatization

Deregulation and privatization have facilitated the entry of new competitors into relatively stable, regulated industries such as energy, airlines, media, trucking, banking, railroads, and telecommunications. In each of these sectors, the enhanced competition has often been associated with the building of excess capacity. In many cases this has dramatically lowered the cost to the consumer, but on the other side it has strained profit margins to the point of forcing a number of major companies into insolvency. Who can forget the bankruptcies of Worldcom, United Airlines, and Enron?

ADJUSTING EXPECTATIONS

Some may consider the forces described above as just signs of the times that will not significantly change the business cycle, corporate profit margins, and balance statements. But these four items relate to serious structural issues that reside outside the traditional cyclical behaviors of the market. As such, they may have a serious impact on the real growth engines of the economy: The corporate profits.

If investments produce lower returns over the long run, this will have a profound ripple effect on financial planning for retirement.

Recently, billionaire Warren Buffet has argued that the years following the bull market of the 1980s, 1990s, and the comeback of 2003 would bring much lower returns. His main point, supported by many other market professionals, is that investors have developed stock market return expectations that are unrealistic, and that we are most likely entering an extended period of market returns that would be well below the much-quoted long-term average return of 10–11 percent.

If investments produce lower returns over the long run, this will have a profound ripple effect on financial planning for retirement. You'll need an increase in lifetime savings and a good plan to maintain your standard of living in retirement.

CHAPTER 15

Managing Your Investments

*F*inancial independence and the necessary wealth creation for retirement hinge upon a successful investment strategy and prudent management of your funds. As with any investment, the main goal is to maximize returns while conserving the principal investment and minimizing risk.

How much time and effort are you willing to put forth in managing your investments, and how much control do you wish to exercise over the investment decisions?

In this chapter we critically assess a range of strategies available to private investors that can help you achieve average or better returns on investments. To begin, ask yourself this question: How much time and effort are you willing to put forth in managing your investments, and how much control do you wish to exercise over the investment decisions? If the answer is little or none, then select and delegate this activity to experts who specialize in investments and financial planning.

RICH RESOURCES FOR THE INDEPENDENT INVESTOR

The information revolution has produced the electronic means for the *average investor* to access the same real-time reservoir of stock market information as the brokers who have investment banks or brokerage firms. All pertinent, up-to-date market information about publicly traded firms is readily accessible online and in print media. Furthermore, the online trading of stocks, bonds, mutual funds, and futures is remarkably simple, amazingly fast, and very secure, with both password protection and encryption of transmissions.

Getting Started

Many excellent books have been written about the key elements of stock investing for the novice investor (find a few of the best listed in Appendix B on page 287). These books introduce the beginning investor to the various types of investments, classify the many investment strategies for buying equities, and describe how to do the sound fundamental and technical analysis that leads to success. Each book covers not only the nuts and bolts of playing the stock market but also describes the subjective thought processes that lie at the core of investing.

Print Resources

The American Association of Individual Investors (AAII) is a non-profit association that provides facts and information about investing to the individual. It publishes a monthly journal with timely articles covering a broad range of investment ideas and is available at a very reasonable subscription rate. Lists of reliable websites,

screens and filters for promising stock selection, general investment strategies, and mutual fund performance are typical topics.
The AAII also sponsors seminars and conference groups through
their network of local chapters. For more information or to subscribe, visit their website at www.aaii.com.

The National Association of Investors Corporation (NAIC)
is another nonprofit organization that offers similar services. It
is best known for a robust website that tracks virtual investment
portfolios for inexperienced investors and high-school investment-
club competitions. The investors begin with a fixed amount
of money to invest, and the performance of their investments
is compared to those of their peers. Find them online at
www.better-investing.org.

Most local libraries subscribe to Standard & Poor (S&P 500)
(www2.standardandpoor.com) and Value Line (1,800 stocks)
(www.valueline.com) publications. These volumes contain massive amounts of data about individual stocks that usually cover
a period of ten to fifteen years and include most items seen on
income and balance sheet statements. Additionally, individual
stocks are given positive or negative ratings depending upon their
performance and growth prospects.

A large number of monthly business magazines fill bookstores
and are available by subscription. Unfortunately, these tabloids
tend to spin business information, project eternal optimism, and
feed the herding instinct that infests Wall Street. The *Wall Street
Journal* (online.wsj.com) and the *Financial Times* (www.ft.com)
are more reliable newspapers and provide comprehensive data and
commentary about all major U.S. and international markets.

Electronic Media

Most publicly owned companies place up-to-date financial statements, annual reports, tax filing, and product information on their websites for their investors and potential investors to review. Additionally, cable and satellite TV have channels that offer continuous business news and current stock market information. Watching the Bloomberg or CNBC business channel can be hypnotic and addictive to the private investor—you can watch the minute-to-minute fluctuations in the Dow, NASDAQ, S&P 500, as well as the price of various commodities and gold and yields on the five-, ten-, and thirty-year Treasury bonds.

With the level playing field created by all this access to information, it is arguable that individual investors can successfully compete with professional money managers and financial advisers.

Find Your Favorite Resources

In a nutshell, these resources for studying and following the market are just a few of those available to any individual who wishes to become a savvy investor. Once you become involved in the market and do your own research, you'll find your own avenues and preferences for keeping up to date. With the level playing field created by all this access to information, it is arguable that individual investors can successfully compete with professional money managers and financial advisers.

INVESTMENT FORMULAS FOR RETIREMENT

General guidelines for investors closer to retirement age differ from those appropriate for younger individuals. In retirement, when your day-to-day cash supply relies heavily on Social Security plus the interest and dividends from your investments, the returns need to be more secure and predictable. A general rule is that the closer you are to retirement and the more dependent you are on your investments to pay current expenses, the less risk you should take with your investments. Government securities and insured bank CDs are some of the least risky investments, with a guaranteed fixed rate of interest and redemption at face value at maturity. Money markets and investment grade corporate bonds also offer above-average safety.

The closer you are to retirement and the more dependent you are on your investments to pay current expenses, the less risk you should take with your investments.

Investment Resource Allocation

Investment resource allocation is a term used to describe how assets are to be divided between cash or cash equivalents, bonds, and stock equities. This formula will vary widely depending upon your age, net worth, current income needs, and tolerance for risk. As age and income needs increase, more is allotted to bonds and cash equivalents. As your net worth and tolerance for risk increase, more is allotted to stock equities. Retirees must also consider other factors such as spending habits, parsimony, and life expectancy. If questions remain, you should consult a financial planner or adviser.

Statistically, during the past fifty years stocks have outperformed bonds and savings certificates by several percentage points. Equities often yield better returns quickly because they involve greater volatility and risk. However, short-term stock prices often narrowly reflect quarterly revenues, profits, and market sentiment—as opposed to longer-term outlook and fundamental analysis. And most growth companies have a low dividend and dividend payout ratio.

No investment is without risk.

All stock portfolios should be diversified to eliminate undo risk in any one or several stocks—basically, don't put all your eggs in one basket. By investing in twenty or more stocks in diverse business segments such as technology, energy, chemicals, manufacturing, health care, and consumer cyclicals, you can ensure that your portfolio will fluctuate up and down in accordance with the general market. Diversification helps to lessen market risk. Capital gains tax and taxes on dividends are lower than the higher tax brackets on current income, thus rewarding profitable equity investments over interest payments; you'll give less to the government in taxes if your money is in the stock market.

No investment is without risk. Government bonds are a case in point. Depending upon many factors—the foremost of which is a decrease or increase by the Federal Open Market Committee (Federal Reserve) in interest rates—government bond prices can widely fluctuate. Bonds that mature far in the future generally command a higher yield, and movements in bond prices go in the opposite directions from interest-rate changes. At a bond's maturity date you will receive the fixed amount for the bond, but if you need to sell before this time, you could receive more or less than the bond's face value.

Investing Styles

Investment experts and managers of large mutual funds often promote different styles of investing; categories include large caps, small caps, growth, value, specialty, sector, and overseas. Remaining faithful to just one style of investing places the typical fund manager at a disadvantage. And as a private investor, you have the option of mixing styles to afford more flexibility and speed to adjust to changing stock market conditions. The fund manager usually has many thousands of shares to buy or sell, and this will adversely influence the market price for that particular stock if done too quickly. Most private investors, however, are not faced with this restraint.

But in all styles of investing there should be an objective evaluation of the company's fundamentals and growth prospects. After doing this homework, you may factor in anything you wish, such as price momentum, intuition, economic indicators, sector performance, analyst's recommendations, technical analysis, hot tips from the cocktail circuit, the outcome of the Super Bowl, and your friendship with the company's senior executives. Just make sure you have reasonable, realistic knowledge about a company before you sink your money into it.

INVESTMENT ADVICE FROM THE EXPERTS

One useful strategy for investing is called the "contrarian" or "value" approach to investing (see Dreman, David. 1998. *Contrarian Investment Strategies* in Appendix B on page 287). This revolves around bottom-fishing for underpriced or out-of-favor stocks with low price-to-earnings ratios, high book values, adequate financial strength, and improving prospects for a turnaround. As part of your research, use the product or service offered by the company to evaluate its quality and get a feel for its marketing prospects (see Lynch, Peter. 1989. *One up on Wall Street* in Appendix B on page 287). It is generally advisable to invest in the types of businesses you understand, so you can appreciate what the data about the company is telling you. Finally, investing in a company should make sense, and your research should reveal a compelling story about why you want to invest in that company.

> *It is generally advisable to invest in the types of businesses you understand, so you can appreciate what the data about the company is telling you.*

There are few investors who have the good luck and intuition to consistently "beat" the market indices. Investing in stocks and bonds is not a get-rich-quick scheme. Day trading, leveraged option buying, drawing on margins, and churning portfolios do not make sense for most individual investors, especially retirees.

Remember: Fundamental analysis is and always should be at the heart of the investing process. Using hot stock tips as the sole basis for investing decisions is hazardous to your financial health.

In the next two chapters, we compare the pros and cons of using money managers as opposed to managing your own investments.

CHAPTER 16

Enlisting the Help of Money Managers

*A*lthough money management is purely a customer service business, exemplary customer service is the exception rather than the rule. Once you lock into a relationship with a firm and complete the initiation process—a process that includes an assessment of your risk tolerance and a model for asset allocation—money managers seem to focus on the size of your account rather than your personal concerns. But, in their defense, many small groups of money managers handle large numbers of customers and many millions, if not billions, of dollars, spread across hundreds of accounts. This may leave them little time to tailor their services to meet the expectations of individual investors.

Management fees are generally fixed, and they decrease as the size of the account increases. Many brokers and financial planners charge too much—as a rule of thumb, the total annual cost should be less than 1.2 percent of your portfolio's value. Some advisers will charge an hourly fee or an annual retainer in place of a percentage of your account. It is important to have a thorough understanding of any and all additional investment expenses.

It's virtually impossible to find a brokerage house or investment bank that will offer to base their fee schedule on performance. Their argument is that their management fees should increase or decrease according to the growth or shrinkage of your account. They contend that this is adequate motivation to be a high performer. Granted, their reputation may suffer from bad years, but this policy is usually very beneficial to them.

Many brokers and financial planners charge too much—as a rule of thumb, the total annual cost should be less than 1.2 percent of your portfolio's value.

However, it's important to note that brokers and financial advisers manage other people's money with no risk to their own personal wealth. For example, say they manage $200 million in assets that generates $2.4 million in fees; if they perform ten percent under comparable market indices, their revenue lowers by only $240,000. It's comparable to a surgeon who has no malpractice risk and gets paid for an operation even if the outcome is unsatisfactory: The unfortunate customer feels the pain, while the manager feels only the embarrassment. Prolonged bear markets always cause unpleasant tensions between advisers and investors, and in the recent past, investors have had ample cause to be dissatisfied.

Investment advisers are clever with numbers, and the more unscrupulous advisers will manipulate their numbers to excuse poor performance. They may exaggerate a convoluted mix of benchmarks and metrics to place the blame solely on market conditions. To combat this, insist that consistent objective benchmarks be used to assess the annual performance of your investing goals when you contract for investment management. Commonly used benchmarks are the performance measures pegged to the thirty Dow industrials, the S&P 500, the NASDAQ 100, the Value Line Index, the Lehman bond indices, or a combination of stock and bond-fund indexes. The performance monitors should reflect the types of stocks you have in your portfolio.

Investment advisers have an obligation to educate their clients on when and why they make stock purchases and sales. Do not allow yourself to be patronized or ignored, and if it's already happening, find a new adviser—it's your money, and you deserve to know what's being done with it. A quarterly or semiannual face-to-face meeting between you and your adviser offers an excellent forum to review progress, adjust resource allocation, and collaboratively manage the account. And you should always be able to call or email with questions or concerns. With smaller firms, it is a nice touch if the client is introduced to the other advisers in the organization who will contribute their expertise to the investment decisions for the account.

Most large investment brokerage firms maintain a secure website that offers market, sector, and company information, as well as links to current news and analyst opinions. Access to these rich information resources allows the investor to be more involved than ever before. Many firms with password-enabled systems allow their clients to view their lists of stocks and valuations in real time.

Money management firms should also perform custodial services for IRAs and reporting functions to the IRS without additional fees.

CHOOSING YOUR MONEY MANAGER

A thorough search for a money manager is usually richly rewarded. Here are a few ideas to help you find a potential financial adviser and gauge their qualifications:

- Make a list of investment firms in your area. In my experience, the best performing advisers come from smaller firms who manage funds of less than four to six hundred million dollars. With a smaller firm, a trusting relationship is easier to nurture, and you are more likely to have some input in investment decisions.

- Check the credentials of the advisers. Are they certified financial planners, chartered financial consultants, financial analysts, certified public accountants, and so on? They should have some specialized training and ample experience.

- Solicit testimonials from friends about their long-standing relationships and experience with money managers, investment banks, brokerage firms, and online trading companies.

- Make certain that the investment adviser/firm is not under investigation or has not had any troubles with the security regulators.

- Be leery of any adviser who promises extraordinary returns.

- Have face-to-face interviews with one or more representatives from the firms you have culled from your initial lists.

- Evaluate the product offerings from all angles. What are the fees, who will service your account, how important is customer service to the firm, and so on?

Use these questions to determine which manager and firm are best suited to meet your needs, and then make the leap of faith and hire them.

A thorough search for a money manager is usually richly rewarded.

Switching Your Money Manager

Switching money managers is often a difficult but necessary decision; if their guidance consistently produces a performance that's under market benchmarks, you should probably take your business elsewhere. Accept the fact that when you ask to transfer an account, there will be paperwork, delays, and some associated transfer fees. However, it will probably make you more money in the long run.

The most important thing, if you're going to pay high fees for money management, is demanding and receiving exemplary customer service. If you're not getting it, try finding a new manager, forcing accountability, or finding more appropriately placed incentives. That should help you get the care and attention you deserve.

CHAPTER 17

Personal Equity Management

*W*hen you retire, your tax-deferred retirement accounts are usually rolled over into IRAs with new management arrangements. When this occurs, retirees with ample free time may wish to take a more active role in personally managing their investments.

You should have a broker or online brokerage house help you meet the federal requirements for transferring these accounts, keep track of their balances and activity, and generate reports on them. But online stock trading makes the buying and selling of stocks and bonds a relatively simple process with modest costs. The trades are usually executed in a matter of seconds and produce consistently fair prices. Stock trading is definitely something you can do on your own, from the comfort of your home computer.

Prudent investment decisions require research and objective evaluation, and this takes time, effort, an ongoing search for market opportunities, and near-constant evaluation of stock performance. Some people find it painfully difficult to make the final buy/sell decisions necessary to manage their portfolios, and generally the overconfident investor and the wishy-washy, equivocator type are not good investors. Overall, some find the intellectual requirements of investing too time-consuming and tedious, and if you feel this way, it is probably wise to delegate investment decisions to the financial professionals.

Many investment advisers would have you believe that investing is an exacting science and requires very specialized knowledge. The implication is that to achieve positive results, you need the services of a true expert. But many independent investors achieve just as good and occasionally better results on their own.

Stock trading is definitely something you can do on your own, from the comfort of your home computer.

In order to successfully manage your stock portfolio, you must keep abreast of the market and follow your investments closely. Appreciate the fact that even though you have a plethora of financial information at your fingertips, many investment decisions come down to intuitive reasoning about incomplete data and uncertain forecasts. But as you gain experience, your results will probably equal those of professional money managers. This is especially true when your investing personality is characterized by humility rather than overconfidence and you thoroughly understand the risk and reward equation.

Other compelling arguments exist for shouldering personal equity management. The most compelling is, of course, your self-interest in doing well—as it's your personal fortune, you'll research each investment as thoroughly as possible and take extreme care in all decisions. Plus, managing your investment decisions is a learning exercise that adds to your understanding of how the U.S. and global economies and businesses function and fit together. And the majority of annual management fees will disappear. You can productively reinvest the money you save.

Finally, personal investors have the advantage of flexibility and speed. You do not have to achieve consensus with other professionals or an investment board or adhere to strict guidelines that corner you into a predetermined type of investing. Individual investors have the latitude to scan a much broader range of investment opportunities. Indeed, studies have shown that portfolio performance is far more dependent upon investor behavior than on a manager's performance.

The bulls and bears on Wall Street exhibit a tendency to herd together and be followers; there exists an air of elite correctness and unconstrained optimism, and they tend to believe too much in what they hear from other Wall Street insiders. Objectively speaking, it is probably wise to ignore all stock recommendations made in business publications and TV programs. Too often hidden agendas are buried in these recommendations, and the price of most publicized picks reflects this vast media exposure by the time you get ready to buy. It's better to buy stocks that are out of fashion but have good fundamentals. Use your educated intuition and critical thinking to pick stock winners.

It's better to buy stocks that are out of fashion but have good fundamentals.

Of course, a simpler option than stock trading is to directly invest in one or more of the galaxy of mutual funds. Investment banks, insurance companies, and brokerage houses sponsor hundreds of large mutual funds with innumerable investment goals and objectives designed to satisfy any type of investor. Index funds invest in a mixture of stocks across the common indices, such as the Dow Jones industrials, NASDAQ, and S&P 500, as well as smaller market segments. For investors with limited funds and those who wish to only peripherally manage their funds, index funds have strong appeal. Index funds essentially eliminate market risk through diversification. However, the income tax on capital gains and dividends within mutual funds also has tax ramifications. Discuss these issues with vendors and advisers.

Timing the Market

It is inadvisable to try to "time the market." Those who try to anticipate moves in the market and time their purchases in sync with these gyrations often forget the fact that timing involves two sets of decisions: When to get in or out, and when to get out or in. It is improbable that both decisions can be made with any degree of accuracy. Just listen to the opinions of the gurus on Wall Street, and you quickly learn why it is folly to base your main investment strategy on forecasting the moves in the stock market—even the expert's opinions are all over the map.

Sensible investors should always monitor and understand their investments. Taking charge can be a profitable and stimulating learning experience. Who better to look after you than yourself?

Managing Everyday Dollars and Possessions

Chapter 18
The Art and Science of Buying and Selling

Chapter 19
A Smooth Inheritance Distribution

The Art and Science of Buying and Selling

*P*rosperity, economic and social stability, astute marketing, marvelous innovation, and pervasive optimism have hooked the majority of Americans born since the Great Depression on material possessions. Discretionary wealth and easy credit fuels the joy of conspicuous consumption. Most of us are tireless shoppers and have evolved window-shopping into an American pastime.

Quite naturally, our appetites for consumption follow us into retirement. But most retirees subsist on fixed incomes, and borrowing is difficult and ill-advised if not matched by earning power or collateral. Thus, our appetites must become more securely tethered to available resources when we retire.

When purchasing behavior is carefully managed, in most instances 20–50 percent fewer dollars can support the same standard of living without undue sacrifice.

With fewer dollars to spend, the retiree often needs to figure out how to maintain a standard of living on less. Intelligent dollar management can usually accomplish this goal. When purchasing behavior is carefully managed, in most instances 20–50 percent fewer dollars can support the same standard of living without undue sacrifice.

EIGHTEEN POSITIVE BUYING HABITS

1. Create an annual budget.

Piece together an annual budget that can be supported by your retirement funds. Review your former monthly incomes and expenditures, and figure out how much, if at all, you need to cut back on spending. If you need to cut, prioritize and eliminate those items that have the least utility and return value. Begin to prospectively plan for major purchases such as cars and home improvements. Once you have formulated a budget, try to adhere to it. Openly discuss variances with your partner. In the first few years of retirement, compare year-to-year results, and make cuts in spending for "wants" rather than "needs." This approach may sound too businesslike, but a family's financial position benefits just as much from budgeting as a business does.

2. Avoid using cash for purchases over $15.

Use check stubs, receipts, and credit card statements to track all purchases. Break down expenses into general categories such as food, car, travel, department store, entertainment, eating out, home maintenance, clothing, taxes, and so on. You must be aware of your expenses before you can manage them, and minimally using cash can help you track effortlessly.

3. Understand your buying personality.

It usually helps you spend wisely if you try to counteract feelings of urgency and immediacy when shopping. Consider your budget and the benefit/cost of each large-ticket item before you buy it. Skilled salesmen, by instilling a sense of deadline and unusual opportunity, try to get customers to purchase before they think. Do not be victimized by high-pressure tactics, and delay the purchase of all major items until a second visit to the store.

4. Avoid credit card debt.
The interest rate on monthly balances is excessive—pay them in full, and cut up all but one or two of your charge cards.

5. Always make shopping lists when you go to the store.
Stay focused on the items you have planned to purchase to minimize impulse buying.

6. Shop only when you're satisfied.
Try to avoid shopping for food when you are hungry or for any item when you are depressed or emotionally upset.

7. Look for real bargains.
Always be on the lookout for bargains, sales, and discounts when searching for necessary items. However, even if items are deeply discounted or part of a seasonal clearance sale, it is not a bargain if they do not produce definable benefits and value. Make sure it's worth the money even if it's not too much money.

8. Use your discounts.
Use senior discounts, coupons, customer discount cards, membership rewards, and frequent-flyer miles to lower costs.

9. Make shopping special.
Shop at establishments that focus on customer service and have employees who are trained to accommodate your special needs.

A business that will walk the extra mile provides real value that enhances the shopping experience and in most instances lowers the total lifetime cost of owning a product, because of responsive service, timely support, and quick complaint resolution.

10. Find everyday bargains.

Shop major discount stores and those stores with *documented,* everyday low prices.

11. Form comparative frames of reference for the prices of individual items.

Try to understand quality differences and appreciate the range of product substitutions available. When you are uncertain about value when making a purchase, research further and sleep on it.

12. If something looks too good to be true, it probably is.

Make sure you have completed your research before proceeding. Online promises such as "it's free," "get rich quick," "miracle cure," "you're a big winner," and other sales hype should raise the red flag of a scam. Sales pitches that promise extraordinary investment returns should raise suspicion. The spigot of telemarketers and email spammers should be turned off, if possible, and ignored. Never reveal your credit card or Social Security numbers to strangers, mystery callers, or websites that are not secure.

13. Sharpen your negotiating skills.

Haggling over price and demanding more for your money may seem impolite and disconcerting. But remember—in an environment of fierce competition, the need to maintain market share forces department stores to heavily rely on clearance sales and deep discounting. With discounting, they lead you to believe that the price on the sales tag is always a fixed price. But in more venues than you might imagine, price is not set in stone and sales persons are allowed to negotiate further discounts and special deals. With a major purchase, this is the case even in large department stores. Insistence on a negotiated deal often produces a lower purchase price, better payment terms, enhanced guarantees, and free add-ons. Haggling, when perfected, is an art form that can be part of the shopping adventure. Furthermore, what do you have to lose when you offer to pay a lower price or request upgrades or additional features for an item? Realize that the markup on retail merchandise is usually 100–300 percent. This provides plenty of wiggle room for the shrewd merchant to profitably lock in a sale by giving the customer an irresistible, discounted purchase price. In particular, use your buying power to get lower prices when merchandise is out of season or the items are slightly defective or used.

14. When contracting for services, seek competing bids from more than one provider.

Ask for references so that, if necessary, you can get live testimonials from others who have used the service. Try to break down all costs and nail down a fixed price. Make certain both you and the vendor have a common understanding about cost overruns and add-ons. Take the time to write down and date the agreed-upon terms to help defend your interests should a dispute arise. This simple documentation, even if sketchy and lacking the vendor's signature, can help you get a favorable settlement if the matter goes to arbitration. Extend this due diligence to a wide range of services such as dental, legal, accounting, tax, home remodeling, driveway sealing, swimming pool care, landscaping, and so on.

15. Research major expenditures before the purchase.

This can be accomplished a number of ways, including an Internet search, consumer magazines, testimonials, product brochures, and comparison shopping. The more you know about a product or service, the better equipped you are to negotiate the best deal. For example, consider buying a new car without visiting a dealer's showroom. If your preliminary research has defined the make, model, and options you want, this type of transaction can be easily accomplished over the telephone or Internet. With just an hour invested, you can have multiple dealers bid and compete for your business. This is a much more efficient and objective way to buy a durable product by exploiting the intense competition between dealers, and it can help get you to a rock-bottom purchase price.

16. Find the best price for your medications.

Prescription medications deserve special mention since they are often a major monthly expense for retirees. Retail pharmacy prices vary greatly, and discount pharmacies are usually more affordable. Compare the prices offered by major pharmacies, and negotiate the price for your long-term medications. Also, discuss drug costs with your doctor, since he can often prescribe a less costly medication and give you free samples. Effective generic (non-branded) medications are tightly regulated by the FDA and much less expensive than the highly promoted proprietary medications. For long-term drugs, consider a mail-order pharmacy plan or purchasing from an outlet in Canada.

17. Find affordable health insurance.

Health insurance is a major expense for retirees. If possible, carry your health plan coverage that is purchased and/or sponsored by your employer into retirement. This often is not an option, since many employers have cut retiree health care benefits to boost their bottom line. Managed care organizations (MCOs) try to hand-pick healthier populations and charge exorbitant premiums for solo or married enrollees who have not reached the age of sixty-five and are without employer health insurance coverage. If you are under sixty-five, shop around since premiums vary widely. If possible, try to join a group purchasing pool like those offered by the local Chamber of Commerce, small business associations, and co-ops. When you reach sixty-five, sign up for Part A and Part B Medicare coverage, and add to it a gap-filler insurance policy to pay the 20 percent of provider fees not covered by Medicare. Joining a managed care plan that accepts Medicare-assigned contracts often provides broader coverage.

18. Shop online.

Internet shopping has seen and will continue to see meteoric growth. Virtually anything—new or used, big or small—can be purchased over the Internet. All major businesses have websites where you can buy almost all of their products. Clothes retailers and bookstores are the best known to the retail customer. These sites are quite user-friendly, and discounts are everywhere on the Web. Security and privacy are guaranteed by the use of passwords and encryption. Identity theft due to a stolen credit card number can happen but probably is a less common occurrence than when you charge at a department store or restaurant.

Astute buying habits are a discipline that is grounded in both art and science. Shopping should be a pleasurable activity. The onus of pressure and stress is on the salesman and business establishment;

you, the buyer, control the process and should demand good service and value. The joy of window-shopping is an acquired taste that can be fine-tuned and interwoven with other social activities. The variety and selection in our American stores is astounding. The eighteen rules above are a framework for discerning buying habits that address the human frailties generally exploited by retailers. Turn the tables in your favor.

SELLING YOUR STUFF

Over the years, literally truckloads of "valuable" clutter accumulate in all the nooks and crannies of your home and storage areas. As a part of the puritanical tradition, Americans save and store anything that might have some future use or is just too sentimental to throw away. Likewise, childhood collections, ordinary household items, artwork, and other treasures with appreciated value may be gathering dust in the attic.

Turn the tables in your favor.

Retirement often brings with it a move to smaller or distant quarters, and this creates an immediate need to completely organize and dispense with many items that can't be squeezed into your new home. The obvious solution is to sell those unneeded items that are salable. Financial needs may also dictate the need to convert your furnishings and collectibles into cash.

First, we must realize that the fundamentals of selling are almost always more difficult to master than those of buying. Most everything you own has a story to tell. Letting go of prized keepsakes is usually attended by a degree of seller's remorse and can make you feel as though you are parting with a piece of yourself. This is especially true of cherished family possessions and handed-down artifacts that have become a part of your family identity.

Letting go of prized keepsakes is usually attended by a degree of seller's remorse and can make you feel as though you are parting with a piece of yourself.

Moreover, selling requires planning. To start with, you must rationally decide what items you can comfortably part with and have a general idea about their dollar value. Often the object must be cleaned, repaired, and readied for sale. Pricing is usually tricky; appraisals are helpful to establish a baseline value.

Unless you engage an agent or a firm to sell or auction the pieces, selling requires that you take an active role in the process. Without formal sales training and experience, most individuals find person-to-person selling stressful and degrading. Granted, there are some gifted extroverts who love the selling experience, but they are the exceptions. Being the seller carries with it a risk of rejection, the blemish of being a merchant, and possible abuse from difficult customers.

OPTIONS FOR SELLING

1. Garage/Yard Sales

America is the land of the weekend garage/yard sale. These sales can include any imaginable item that's partially functional or decorative. Few items are in mint condition, and most have already been offered to and refused by family members.

There is a huge following for garage sales. Most addicted patrons are looking for antique treasures that can be bought for a song because the seller is unaware of the underlying value. A Tiffany vase, collectible toys and dolls, or historic prints are examples of items that look grungy in garage sales but may be found to have considerable value after cleaning.

Other followers are young couples looking for secondhand items on the cheap to furnish an apartment or care for a home and garden. Whatever the case, garage sales are basically giveaways for unneeded clutter that is too good to put into the dumpster. The amount collected is rarely substantial, and if lucky, you realize about ten cents on a dollar of replacement costs. However, this can be an easy and fun way to get rid of possessions that aren't all that valuable but that someone else might want or need.

2. Auction Houses

Local, regional, and international auction firms have loaned a new convenience and clarity to the process of selling fine collectibles. Auction houses create a level playing field that helps hobbyists and estate managers get an amount that approaches the true replacement market value for their treasures. For most individuals with no insider connections to or working knowledge of the tangibles market, auction houses let you sell your marketable valuables with fairness and ease.

Each auction house varies in the type of goods they specialize in, and fee schedules vary but are usually negotiable. In most instances, despite the recent price-fixing scandals involving major auction houses, these establishments have an incentive to maximize the selling price since fees are generally a percentage of the sales price. To avoid the low-ball bidder, a minimum reserve price (lowest price that will be accepted) can be set by the seller.

The tangibles dealers throughout the United States despise the auction houses.

To verify the service offered by the auction houses, consider the fact that the tangibles dealers throughout the United States despise the auction houses. Auction houses have taken away their access to collectibles and tangibles that historically they were able to buy at a fraction of their worth.

3. Online Selling

The dot-com revolution ushered in a new way of buying, selling, and trading. Websites like eBay facilitate the buying and selling of just about anything between individuals online. They afford a secure infrastructure for auction-type competitive and fixed-bid selling, and they help open up the market and match many thousands of buyers and sellers. Getting started in online selling can be simple—sites like eBay, Amazon.com, and Craigslist.com make it easy for anyone to set up an account and start selling. There is a nuisance factor in online selling, however. You must post the item to your webpage, monitor the sale, arrange the exchange, and package and ship the item. But also, you typically get a good price. This can be a very effective and profitable way to sell your unwanted possession, and particularly if they appeal to a niche collectors' market, such as old toys or baseball cards.

4. Direct Selling to Dealers

Major New York and local dealers in artwork, estate jewelry, rugs, antiques, gold, and coins often purchase from private individuals and estates. Usually the amount offered for heirlooms and marketable items is obscenely low. To sell directly to a dealer successfully, you must research and be fully versed in the market of what you plan to sell. No dealer is likely to do you a favor, and the two words that best describe the wholesale dealer and tangibles market are "unscrupulous" and "predatory."

If you are not an active member within the tight-knit fraternity that trades in a specific collectible, or do not have a close advisery relationship with an expert in that field, you should invest in that variety of collectible only because you enjoy owning it. Only in rare instances will you be able to sell your investment for a significant profit, even at a much later date. With few exceptions, collectibles are easy to buy and easy to have appraised at extreme valuations but very difficult to sell at reasonable valuation within the trade.

All appraisals should contain a detailed, precise description of the item. Unfortunately, the vast majority of formal written appraisals contain wording that is fuzzy, inexact, and laden with general descriptors that defy precise interpretation. They often do not serve to minimize insurance premium expense or guarantee suitable equivalent replacement in the event of loss. This deficiency may relate to many factors, but for the most part, the neglect of appraisal detail is quite intentional. Tangible collectibles are essentially blind items for most owners, and dealers exploit this vulnerability and asymmetry of information.

> ## *The two words that best describe the wholesale dealer and tangibles market are "unscrupulous" and "predatory."*

It is eye-opening when you first come to understand that there is little relationship between appraisal value and market value. An appraisal may authenticate an item but is often worthless in selling fine goods. There are four basic types of appraisals:

- Appraisal for Insurance Purposes: These are usually highly inflated to give the buyer the reassurance that he has made an excellent purchase, and to provide both the retailer and insurance carrier plenty of wiggle room should the item need to be replaced due to theft, loss, or damage. For instance, if the wholesale replacement cost of a diamond ring is $2,500, an insurance appraisal might estimate its value at $6,000. If an insurance claim is made due to loss, the ring can be replaced for $2,500, but the retail jeweler can bill the insurance company $5,000 (a standard markup of 100 percent). In this transaction, the jeweler makes a profit of $2,500 and still saves the insurance company $1,000, since the insurance company does not have to pay the full amount of the retail appraised value. The customer is the loser since he has been paying an average insurance premium of $66 annually to insure $6,000 worth of jewelry. In replacement he has received less than 50 percent of the insured value.

- Retail Appraisals: These usually mirror insurance appraisals, with an estimated retail cost that ranges between 100 and 300 percent above wholesale cost. This likewise gives the customer the impression that they received a fair deal and bought right, which might not be the case.

- Replacement Cost or Wholesale Cost: This is the best indicator of true value, since this is the price the retail jeweler would pay. An accurate appraisal for insurance purposes that reflects this intrinsic value should take this figure and add 20–40 percent.

- Pawn Shop, Estate, or Dealer Appraisal: This defensive type of appraisal places the lowest absolute dollar amount on an item. This low figure serves several interested parties. First, it places the lowest value on an estate to avoid tax. Second, it is a figure at which an item can be turned into instant cash. Third, this figure enables the item to be sold by a dealer to another dealer at a profit.

5. Personal Selling

Trading-post tabloids, newspaper advertisements, direct-contact marketing, and "for sale by owner" signs are frequently used to sell both large- and small-ticket items. Used cars, residential real estate, pool tables, safes, electronics, and most any item can be marketed directly to the buyer without incurring any fees from an intermediary or agent. Personal selling, however, takes time and effort as well as the inconvenience and nuisance of being available. But often, perseverance and a smooth negotiating style fetch a market price that makes the effort quite worthwhile.

6. Barter, Swaps, and Matching Exchanges

The primitive barter system of direct negotiation and quid-pro-quo exchange still exists in informal trading. It can be creatively used in a manner that benefits both parties, minimizes the tax consequences, and lowers transaction costs.

When calculating wealth to support retirement spending, few people consider that their possessions can play a significant role in the formula. But tangible assets do have intrinsic value, and there are avenues to convert them to cash or cash equivalents. Disciplined selling can help you pad your wallet and live better on less.

CHAPTER 19

A Smooth Inheritance Distribution

*F*amily artifacts usually have sentimental value, tell a story about earlier times, and may also have intrinsic resale value. In most instances, distributing family keepsakes and heirlooms to your children makes more sense than going through the hassle of selling them for a pittance to strangers or a dealer.

Distributing family treasures to your heirs is often more complicated than you would like it to be.

But even if you try to be fair, distributing family treasures to your heirs is often more complicated than you would like it to be. For instance, consider how many of your acquaintances have felt short-changed because of the way in which the family's tangible possessions were distributed. It seems that regardless of the good intentions and generosity of the parents, sibling rivalry has a habit of resurfacing to complicate the process. Often, long-buried slights, feelings of entitlement, and alleged "promises" wreak havoc with family relationships. To circumvent some of these problems, consider the following ideas.

- If your goal is to maintain loving relationships between your children, make fairness, openness, and even-handed treatment a high priority in dispersing family artifacts.

- The owner alone should make the decisions as to who will receive what, when, and under what circumstances. If manipulative behaviors have historically been a problem within the family, the heirs should be notified only after the owner has made the final decisions.

- All possessions, once distributed, should have no strings or conditions attached.

- Possessions should not be used as bargaining chips to exert power and control over the children and grandchildren.

- If an item is promised to someone, a written record should be kept. Some people even put a tag or mark on the item.

- Disciplining a family member for transgressions by cutting him or her off will rarely change errant behaviors, and it usually poisons the relationship forever. It should be avoided.

- Distribution may be complicated by an established family business or control of a privately owned business. Be cautious about relinquishing control prematurely, since divorce, sibling rivalry, and reporting relationships can destroy a family enterprise. Also, these decisions carry complex tax ramifications. It is wise to proactively consult your legal advisers to weigh all options.

Giving away your treasures is tricky and can create discord and hurt feelings that muddy family relationships. Try to find a distribution plan that minimizes family conflict while carrying out your wishes.

Guidelines for Distribution

Before you begin, create a consistent philosophy of estate giving that fits with your desires. These general guidelines should mesh with the expectations you have nurtured within the family. Employ one or more of the following approaches to distributing your wealth:

- An open and clearly stated policy of equal distribution to each child, family, partner, or grandchild.

- A distribution based upon the financial needs of each family member.

- An increased distribution to caregivers and companions upon whom you depended in the declining years.

- A legally documented inheritance plan to donate to charity and the community.

TRIMMING THE FAT

Much of the old stuff in your storage bins is just that: Old stuff. It has no sale or hand-me-down value, and the kids have probably sorted through it repeatedly and have found no use for it. The best you can do is to pitch it or give it to charity. Taking the time to go through it, pull out the usable items, and donate them to an appropriate charity can produce real value for the underprivileged and needy, as well as a tax deduction.

Before tossing anything out, do some research.

But some family heirlooms and even garage sale items have considerable resale and gifting value. It is often said, "One man's junk is another man's treasure." The varied assortments of antique memorabilia with astronomical values that surface on the *Antiques Road Show* TV program give credence to this thesis. Before tossing anything out, do some research.

SECTION VI:

Medical Advancements and Retirement

Chapter 20
Biomedical Discoveries

Chapter 21
Retirement: The Longest of Life's Chapters?

Biomedical Discoveries

*M*edical science is beginning to zero in on the mysteries of aging. It is conceivable that during the twenty-first century, treatments will emerge for cellular aging that slow the process and potentially repair some of the damages of everyday wear and tear.

The rate of scientific discovery is accelerating in a broad spectrum of scientific disciplines including genetics, cellular biology, immunology, virology, and intracellular protein synthesis. Manipulating gene fragments and messenger ribonucleic acid (RNA), as well as the manufacturing of monoclonal antibodies, have helped scientists replicate many enzymes, hormones, antibodies, and cellular proteins that are known to lie at the heart of cellular function and immune response.

Medical science is beginning to zero in on the mysteries of aging.

Stem cells are being cultured that can differentiate into almost any type of mature human cell. This may open the door to growing normal tissue cells that can be injected into the human body to replace poorly functioning or damaged tissues, and can actually produce organs for human transplantation. It is predicted that xeno-organ transplants from genetically modified pigs and other animals that are not rejected by the recipient will become standard practice within ten years. This encouraging development would make up for the enormous shortfall in organ donations.

With great regularity, arthritic joints are being replaced with well-engineered prostheses that allow a full range of motion and a return to normal activities. Mechanical pumps to assist or even replace the heart are entering advanced clinical trials.

Thousands of promising compounds that treat all sorts of disease are in clinical trials. Some are targeted to delay or even reverse conditions that historically were considered the irreversible degenerative conditions of normal aging. New information technology supports the massive number crunching and data mining necessary to control, manage, and store the colossal amount of information generated by this explosion in the medical sciences.

A BETTER QUALITY OF LIFE

The era of medical cures for infectious disease dawned in 1929 with the discovery of penicillin by Alexander Fleming. This resulted in a leap in life expectancy by saving children and young people from lethal microbial disease. The benefits to mankind from antibiotics were startling, and our current massive investments in biomedical research will likely produce another dramatic increase in life expectancy. If these exciting new medical discoveries are coupled with a greater emphasis on preventative medicine and a healthy lifestyle, the twenty-first century will most certainly produce an improved quality of life for older individuals.

Our current massive investments in bio-medical research will likely produce another dramatic increase in life expectancy.

If this occurs, profound social change must follow the dramatic increase in life expectancy. How will an average lifespan of one hundred years influence the cycling of family life and the passing of the baton from generation to generation? How will it influence the workplace, and what will become the standard age for retirement? How will it alter and realign the nation's entitlement plans, taxes, system of health care, volunteerism, and family planning?

Science and Ethics

This brewing cauldron of medical innovation and new therapies has momentum, and many of these advancements raise serious ethical issues that challenge traditional cultural and religious values. Should human cloning studies be permitted and stem cells be used to treat medical disease? With scarce health care dollars, how much is society willing to pay for treatment that produces one quality year of life, and what if rationing of health care becomes a necessity? With the dawn of genetic engineering, should we condone eugenics to improve the genetic makeup of any individual, his or her offspring, or the entire human race? How do we guarantee the privacy of medical information in the Information Age? How do we ensure that all Americans have equal access to quality health care?

None of these ethical dilemmas is easily resolved, and there are staunch supporters on both sides of each issue. In the future, social and cultural ethics will play an increasing role in the national debate, and it will become increasingly difficult to separate ethical issues from medical discovery, party politics, and societal forces.

Rising Life Expectancy

If left unfettered, few investigators would dispute the ultimate and definitive ability of science to discover the fundamental origins of life and thoroughly unravel the workings of the human body. Demographers already project progressive increases in the percentage of senior citizens, and census figures show that the fastest growing segment of U.S. society is centenarians—by the year 2050, centenarians will probably number close to 840,000. And life expectancy may increase more swiftly than is currently forecast. It is conceivable that the most rapidly growing segment in the population might become the 110–120-year group, and the joke that "happiness is dying at the hands of a jealous lover at age ninety" may need to be rewritten to 110.

TWENTY-FIRST CENTURY MEDICINE

It is difficult to predict how the practice of medicine and the medical system will change over the next century. Patient advocacy, better information systems, and electronic medical records will result in improved documentation and communication between patient and doctor. Preventive, predictive, and lifestyle medicine will assume as much importance for the practicing physician as the treatment of disease. With increased patient expectations, physician practices will evolve into service-oriented organizations that provide a greater focus on holistic medicine. Information technology will be used to improve quality, minimize medical mistakes, and insure continuity of care.

Preventive, predictive, and lifestyle medicine will assume as much importance for the practicing physician as the treatment of disease.

"Telemedicine" via online videoconferencing will provide more constant care for homebound patients. Patients will probably carry their complete medical histories with them on smart cards, implanted computer memory chips, hand-held devices, or medical bracelets. Data mining will be used to forecast risks and develop standards of care.

Annual screening exams might become a routine that consists of:

- A risk-factor review imputed and evaluated by a computer program

- A total-body scan that takes one to two minutes to perform and produces a three-dimensional anatomical picture of all major organ systems

- Automated blood tests and cell analysis that gives a comprehensive snapshot of body physiology, tissue enzymatic function, tumor markers, and even a genetic profile that evaluates susceptibility to disease

- A computer-generated report containing all the above information, read by the doctor and used to treat the patient using standardized protocols

From a medical perspective, it is an exciting time in which to live! If you can remain healthy and stay standing for twenty-five or even ten more years, medical help is on the way to relieve, arrest, or retard most of the miseries that today are considered the compost of growing old. Twenty years ago, at age thirteen, my son announced that he was going to live to age 120. I brushed off his comment as childhood fantasy. Now I am not so sure, and the coming years may bring this dream much closer to reality.

CHAPTER 21

Retirement:
The Longest of Life's Chapters?

*T*homas Perls, in his book *Living to Be One Hundred,* concludes that "the oldest old are a select group of individuals who 'get over the hump' because they are able to delay illness at the end of their lives—to compress morbidity." Indeed, with a focus on healthy lifestyles and preventative medicine, plus the efficacy of new medical treatments, it seems reasonable that individuals will remain healthier and more functional into the far reaches of old age. It has been theorized that healthier populations compress the period of serious illness leading to death—they don't succumb to the ravages of preventable and treatable diseases such as hypertension, obesity, diabetes, arteriosclerosis, and late-stage cancers—and as a consequence they lower the overall lifetime costs of medical care. In other words, they die due to the natural aging process.

It seems reasonable that individuals will remain healthier and more functional into the far reaches of old age.

If early retirement and increasing longevity continue, the years beyond employment may equal or even exceed those of employment. The "second half" may truly be a second half. The milestones in life may become the celebration of a seventy-fifth wedding anniversary, the birth of great-grandchildren, and the one hundredth birthday. And as this population segment explodes, the sheer numbers alone will bestow enormous political clout that should frustrate any attempt to curtail entitlement programs.

Our democratic institutions must change to accommodate this demographic shift. Public policy and cultural change should be molded to better capture and utilize this vast pool of talent, energy, and experience. Businesses should consider creating flexible job descriptions, cross-training, lateral transfers, job-sharing, and temporary status that enables a worker to gradually ratchet down the physical and emotional demands of work. Career pathways should facilitate coasting into retirement with a staged transition that encourages the senior to stay on the job.

As well as traditional work, the United States boasts an enormous army of volunteers that support about 1.6 million not-for-profit organizations in America. These programs should be encouraged to fill the gap left by the devolution of public assistance from the federal, state, and local governments over the past twenty years with retired volunteers.

THE EFFECTS OF EARLY RETIREMENT

In an open-market economy, profit, shareholder value, and competitive advantage preempt most other concerns. Job security fluctuates with the short-term revenues and profits of the firm, while the workforce is constantly churned by mergers, acquisitions, outsourcing, downsizing, and restructuring.

Business schools teach that mentoring, teamwork, trust, and loyalty are the essential ingredients for success in business—but the drivers in the business world are change, flexibility, and corporate goals, and a corporation must be agile, lean, and sometimes uncompassionate to succeed. Workers' trust, loyalty, and teamwork get buried in this environment of predatory behavior. The workforce is more and more an expendable commodity. And as a result, layoffs and job switching have increased, along with unexpected early retirement before the worker is adequately prepared.

Forces that encourage early retirement have also hit small-business proprietors and professionals. Lacking scope and scale, small businesses are increasingly under assault from big-box competitors like Wal-Mart and Target. This frequently makes the small proprietor have to run faster just to keep up. Liability and medical insurance costs have escalated, and this drives the hiring of temporary workers to escape paying for fringe benefits. The worker must work harder, receive fewer benefits, and not dally.

All these forces lead to many people retiring early, a phenomenon that has to change—people are living far past age sixty-five and will only be living longer. You need to be more prepared for retirement before it begins than you did thirty years ago, and society has to find ways to utilize the elderly so that they can continue to contribute and grow.

The Social Security Crisis

The burgeoning number of senior citizens is widely discussed in the media and among political groups. In 1985 there were three U.S. workers for every retired person. Now it's close to even. And in 2010, the first of the baby-boomers will hit sixty-five. This will likely leave the United States with a relatively small number of gainfully employed individuals shouldering a seemingly unsustainable burden of paying for the rising costs of retirees. A realist would have to conclude that it is only a matter of time before Social Security and Medicare will go bust.

In 2010, the first of the baby boomers will hit sixty-five.

The fact is that Social Security trust funds have been depleted by years of fiscal immoderation and piracy. Indeed, all actuarial projections, regardless of rosy assumptions that postpone the day of reckoning, point to an impending financial disaster. But messing with Social Security is perilous for an elected official's political health; the entitlement programs are a hot button, and no politician wants to appear unsympathetic to the aging folks by sponsoring programs that cut benefits or significantly raise the age of qualification. Despite the snowballing debt, most new legislation continues to contribute to rising entitlement costs, and Republicans and Democrats alike are considering universal health care plans that will greatly add to the Medicare and Medicaid budgetary shortfalls. This tug of war over dollars will be one of the thorniest in the years to come.

This is yet another reason that society has to find ways for our elderly to work comfortably as eighty million baby-boomers reach retirement age during the next decade.

PHYSICAL AND MENTAL CAPABILITIES

Human physical strength and endurance, when plotted against age, produces a relatively asymmetric bell-shaped curve; it rapidly ascends, plateaus for about fifteen years and then steadily declines. Physical capabilities peak at about age twenty-five, and a steady decline begins around age forty, with some acceleration in this process after age fifty.

The memory files and hard-wiring of the brain are very durable.

Memory and mental acuity seem more resistant to the decline of advancing age than physical capabilities. Most of us do experience some decrease in the speed with which we can actively recall and process information, which accounts for the "senior moments" that we all experience. But in general the memory files and hard-wiring of the brain are very durable.

Much has been written about emotional intelligence and social skills in recent years. Strong social skills have been shown to be an excellent predictor of success in a new job—it is good advice to "hire the smile, train the worker." Some individuals are naturally gifted in getting along with people, while for others emotional intelligence is a skill acquired by practice and training. And these social graces and affective skills are very resistant to decay.

Finally, the insight and know-how of experience adds an important dimension to the repertoire of the senior set. We learn from both our successes and mistakes, and it is often said that a good experience is valuable, but a bad experience is invaluable. The learning process continues throughout life, and experience nurtures intuition that serves as the internal compass with which we make wise decisions.

When we look in the aggregate at these four human performance categories—physical capabilities, memory and mental acuity, emotional intelligence, and experience—it tells us that in aging, with the exception of physical capabilities, we see a remarkably slow decline in performance. This begs the question: How can we better utilize these durable capabilities?

We will seek some answers in the final chapters.

SECTION VII:

Some Great New Activities for Retirement

CHAPTER 22

Computers and the Internet

*E*lectronic technology is for the young, or so it would appear when watching a five-year-old skillfully navigate the intricacies of a computer game. With early exposure to the world of electronic devices, young people develop a natural bond with the computer. Indeed, working with computers and electronic games from an early age produces a certain hard-wiring of the brain that jump-starts hand-eye coordination and reflexes.

The most common and useful computer applications can be mastered by most anyone, young or old.

Nevertheless, computer skills are learned skills. Computer programs and applications require multiple simple steps in the proper sequence to achieve an objective. The basic process is the same whether you are creating a customized Christmas card or designing a jet engine. The most common and useful computer applications can be mastered by most anyone, young or old. Moreover, the determination, patience, and frustration tolerance that characterize middle age and beyond make the computer no match for a tenacious elder.

In the late 1940s, television was the new thing. It is difficult for young people even to understand that those of us over age sixty survived a time during childhood without television. These days, without question, the wide variety of television programming affords a significant diversion and dimension to retirement. And individuals who like watching television at home in a comfy easy chair can see an infinite variety of shows for a low monthly cable- or satellite-service fee. Yet television is not interactive, and the viewer is passive. Television programming generally reflects Nielsen ratings and not content quality. It consists of about 25–30 percent bothersome commercial advertisements along with small doses of intellectual stimulation. In contrast to television, the computer, with a few clicks of the mouse, can open an unlimited world of information and entertainment that is tailored to one's personal preferences.

THE BENEFITS OF BEING ONLINE

Standards of living after retirement vary widely between the rich and poor, and accordingly, options for leisure activities must be pegged to the pocketbook. But the benefits from computer technology are relatively inexpensive and flow freely to virtually all socioeconomic classes. For less than $800 and a modest Internet service provider (ISP) monthly fee, any trainable and motivated individual can enjoy the full wonders of the wired world on a leading-edge computer system. And most desktop and laptop computers have loads of memory and storage capacity with at least a 200-gigabyte hard drive (one gigabyte equals 1,000 megabytes, and one megabyte equals about three hundred pages of typewritten text) and 1–2 gigabytes of rapid access memory, or RAM.

Although it can be intimidating, mastering the basics of a computer system is not complicated. If the system's applications are properly explained, it should allay any doubts you may harbor about using computers. The basics just take some time and effort, a touch of tenacity, plus a little handholding and encouragement from tech-savvy friends. Often, seniors can engage their children or grandchildren as teachers.

The computer and the Internet are dazzling innovations that open up new vistas for retirees. On the Internet you can access up-to-date information about virtually any subject—history, science, geography, the Yellow Pages, government agencies, educational facilities, volunteer opportunities, stock markets, businesses, and e-commerce. Email, chat rooms, blogs, and videoconferencing enable instant communications with anyone most anywhere in the world. Most products and services can be bought and sold online, and even large-ticket items such as antique cars, artwork, and homes have exchanged hands over the Net. You can bank, file your income taxes, price-compare mortgages on a new home, trade stocks, and do part-time work from almost any remote location on the globe. Software programs support creative expression such as graphic design, movie-making, photographic touch-up, greeting-card design, landscaping, and creative interior home decorating. Voice over the Internet (VOI) and video calls are commonplace using free downloadable software. Interactive computer games as simple as solitaire and as complex as virtual reality games and championship sport contests are designed to meet any taste and skill level. The list of computer options and capabilities just keeps growing.

One of the foremost complaints from middle-management retirees is that they miss having a secretary to handle day-to-day routine matters. Up to a point, a computer can be a surrogate for a secretary. It can simplify bookkeeping, manage phone and mailing lists, and speed information transfer. Be that as it may, the computer doesn't fix coffee, make social appointments, answer the phone, or accept responsibility when things go badly.

> *Often, seniors can engage their children or grandchildren as teachers.*

Broadband with fast transmission rates enables real-time (live) image streaming. Interactive teleconferencing between distant conference locations or multiple family members is becoming commonplace. A new discipline of telemedicine is already evolving and will likely become a part of the average doctor's day-to-day routine within ten years. And with the miniaturization of electronic gadgets through existing chip technology and nanotechnology, plus wireless connectivity, anyone can take the wired world in his or her pocket or purse and connect to anyone who is available from anywhere and at any time. The iPhone is just one of the many gadgets that allows you to access the Internet from just about anywhere.

COMPUTER LITERACY

The use of computers requires your continuous concentration and interaction. As the user, you are in charge of making the device perform. Computer software programs are downloaded into the computer and contain applications that make the computer carry out your commands. When working on the computer, you need to know what you wish to accomplish and how the application or program works to enable you to carry out the task. In general, all computer applications seem awesome and complicated when you first use them, but practice, of course, breeds familiarity and proficiency. And after successfully using and understanding one or more applications, you begin to understand the logic flow and rules behind "computerese." As your computer skills grow, the learning curve to master new programs shortens.

After successfully using and understanding one or more applications, you begin to understand the logic flow and rules behind "computerese."

If you consider the world of technology foreign, hostile, and un-inviting, your feelings are not atypical of many in the senior set. But a compelling case can be made for all retirees to familiarize themselves with the capabilities of computers and then go on to become computer literate. Take the plunge, and spread the word about the computer world.

Useful Computer Applications

Word Processing

Mastering a word processing program is a good starting point—learning the basics within a program such as Microsoft Word provides a foundation to understanding all computer programs. A word processor is like having a typewriter that automatically formats the page, checks the spelling and grammar, provides a thesaurus, and stores a master file copy that can be modified at any time. Word processing is used whenever you generate text documents, so you can use it for letter writing, grocery lists, tracking expenses, etc.

Storing Data

Computers provide excellent storage for any sort of list. This might include addresses, phone numbers, recipes, collections, birthdays, jewelry, insurance inventories, and personal schedules. This eliminates the need for paper storage. The lists are easily updated, accessed, emailed to friends, and printed out onto paper.

Computer Games

There are computer games for all skill levels and tastes, and you can play against the computer or online competitors. Games you likely already know and love such as bridge, chess, and checkers can be played against online opponents, and hundreds of interactive programs like World of Warcraft or Second Life can challenge your quick-thinking skills and hand-eye coordination.

Scanners and Digital Photography Storage

Remarkably affordable and user-friendly digital cameras and scanners can upload any document, photograph, film, or video upload the computer. Photography programs enable you to edit, touch up, enhance, and reproduce photos. Movie-making programs enable you to easily edit digital video clips and add music and titles, and design and visual effect programs enable you to produce any intricate design or animated effect. Computers provide a complete photo lab and movie studio with instant service at nominal cost.

Printers

Inkjet and laser printers are inexpensive and can create a black-and-white or color hard copy from any computer file, or directly from a scanner or other peripheral device. You can print high-resolution photographs onto photo paper that look just as good as the kind produced in a store.

Sharing Computer Files

Computer files can be copied and shared with others via email, printed hard copy, CD-ROMs, detachable hard drives, and in many online venues.

Internet Service Provider (ISP)

Service providers, for a monthly fee, bring you the Internet via phone line, cable, or wireless connection.

The Internet

The Net or Web opens up a world of information. To log in, you access your ISP through an Internet browser that comes loaded on the computer, such as Internet Explorer or Firefox. From there, you can check your email, shop, run searches for information on Google.com or Yahoo.com, read the *New York Times,* and so much more.

CD/DVD Player

A computer can play music and video and, if equipped with an electronic eye, capture video directly. Most computers come with the capability to make copies of DVDs and music and store them on multiple hard drives that are portable and can be used with other computers.

CASE STUDY: COMPUTERS AND RETIREES

Ruth, a retired executive secretary, kept in touch with a circle of friends from college and work by exchanging Christmas cards that included handwritten notes each year. In 2002, she decided to streamline the process and save money with a new computer. She designed and created a personalized Christmas card on the computer, then added a one-page Christmas message that she crafted using a word processor. She customized it by adding a colored border and a clip-art image of Rudolph. She left a space at the bottom of the card for a brief, personalized handwritten message. With the 150 cards she sends yearly, she saves the cost of all those Christmas cards and a full day's work. Moreover, the cards convey a special cordiality and better reflect her personal tastes.

Last year Ruth encouraged her circle of friends to electronically exchange email addresses, telephone numbers, children's names and birthdays, and special recipes. These were compiled as a list in the Microsoft Excel program and shared electronically with the group. This prompted a raft of email messages circulating between the old college gang, keeping each other appraised of current events. On occasion, messages were sent to all group members simultaneously with one simple click of the mouse. As a result of the heightened communication, the group has grown closer together. Recently, they set a date for a reunion, made travel arrangements online, and coordinated plans by email. The open communication afforded by the computer and Internet has rekindled relationships from the past.

Mark, a recent retiree, wanted to look back and create a family lineage tree. He used a computer program to produce the template for the family tree. He added as many relatives as he could remember and then emailed and snail mailed computer-generated copies to other members of the family to solicit further additions. Family records showed that some ancestors had lived in Lancaster, Pennsylvania, and others came from Falmouth, England. Using search engines, Mark found websites for these two communities that gave historic and genealogical data. Fortified with several leads in each community, he later visited them and was able to extend the family tree back two additional generations. Mark's final iteration of the family tree is now an important part of each family's album and matches up many old, faded photographs with names and stories.

Mildred had crippling arthritis and poorly controlled diabetes that caused her to retire early. She had leg pain when she walked more than fifty yards, and due to visual problems she had to give up driving alone. The computer has become her link to the outside world. She exchanges email with friends to keep in touch. She has mastered online stock trading and uses the Internet to purchase books, clothing, medical supplies, and music. She banks and pays her bills online. One niece and two nephews are avid fans of computer games, so she downloads some of the latest action games to challenge them during their frequent visits. Recently, she enrolled in a hospital program for health monitoring in the home. She sends the graph of her daily blood sugar electronically to the hospital and receives email management instructions. She has started to write the family history using a word processor and plans to give each family member a hard copy and a copy on CD. Her collection of family photos has been reproduced using a high-definition scanner, and she has given copies to her brothers and sister. Her computer center has become the command post of her life that keeps her active, amused, connected, and in a position to give back to those she loves.

Arthur didn't retire at age forty-five; he was laid off with inadequate retirement benefits. He is actively seeking employment. He has crafted a personal website on which he has published his curriculum vitae (CV), a list of qualifications and personal interests, and a hyperlink to a video interview. He reads the *New York Times, Wall Street Journal,* and *Cincinnati Enquirer* online each morning, looking for job opportunities. He has emailed his CV to many employers in the area with inquiries about their hiring needs. Recently, he used an online employment agency to help him find work and found many opportunities online that he hadn't seen in print sources.

LEARNING COMPUTER SKILLS

There are many resources for learning basic computer skills. Many public libraries, senior centers, churches, colleges, high schools, job training programs, senior learning classes, and even some businesses offer introductory courses, usually at little or no cost to the student. And family members and friends are usually quite willing to help troubleshoot any glitches you may encounter.

However, most computer geeks will tell you that they were self-trained. Most computer skills come from a trial-and-error process—the learning curve corresponds to the amount of time you spend working with the computer. And when you become comfortable with computers, you will someday wonder how you were once able to get along without their amazing functionality.

CHAPTER 23

Travel

*R*emember those long, hot summer days of your childhood during school break, when you were unfettered and could roam the neighborhood on your bike, just following the dial of your creative compass? Well, retirement can be the reincarnation of that rare and joyous period in our lives. You are on an extended holiday that invites creative wanderings and adventure without time constraints.

An urge to be on the road to explore new destinations and visit family and old friends highlights the early years of retirement. Travel is a chance to break with your usual routine and get exposure to a fresh environment. It can clear the mind and nourish the soul.

THE JOY OF TRAVEL

Travel uniquely expands intellectual horizons. Videos and polished travel-club presentations fall short in capturing the flavor and adventure of actually being there, observing the subtleties of a different culture firsthand, and independently forming your own opinions. Mingling with foreign nationals teaches you respect for their way of life. There is no real substitute for seeing original artwork in foreign museums and visiting ancient sites. A movie about the ruins at Pompeii does not capture the catastrophic event like being there does.

Without the encumbrances of home and the comfort of the usual routine, travel frees your mind to reflect on where you have been in life. In my own experience, time away without distraction seems to enrich even your dreams, making early memories come to life and heightening creative thinking. There is nothing like a walk on the beach with the rhythm of the waves in the background for reflection and introspection, and to facilitate problem solving.

In my own experience, time away without distraction seems to enrich even your dreams.

For individuals seeking new friendships and exposure to an interesting assortment of people, travel offers rich opportunities. Most tours and many resorts have social programs designed to promote social mixing; most regimented travel groups such as cruises and tours offer activities that promote easy introduction of guests with diverse backgrounds. I have seen many deep friendships develop on tours and in two instances the development of an enduring relationship.

Traveling with a few friends or couples in your social circle also has advantages. The men can have golf partners and the women shopping buddies (or vice versa), and you can share the cost of a good vintage wine at dinner. Additionally, these joint activities can be switched on or off and do not have to interfere with your independent agenda.

CHANGING EXPECTATIONS

As youngsters, most of us enjoyed sleeping in sleeping bags under a tent on hard, cold ground. In those days a campfire and the great outdoors made even a hot dog on a dry bun taste delicious.

Noisy campers, lack of sleep, smelly latrines, and cold showers were merely par for the course. As a teenager or even young adult, a train ride across the country; a red-eye plane flight, the bunkhouses of youth hostels; bland, greasy edibles; and irregular mealtimes were totally acceptable.

Maturity, affluence, and travel finesse change your definition of convenience and creature comforts.

However, maturity, affluence, and travel finesse change your definition of convenience and creature comforts and upgrade your travel plans to those that offer greater comfort and meet more extravagant expectations. Business-class air travel and stays at major hotels have become the standard. You've become accustomed to staying at resorts with indoor swimming pools, saunas, complete exercise facilities, and tennis courts. There is a gift shop conveniently located in the lobby for the purchase of newspapers, candy bars, books, and anything else you might need. And most rooms offer a large bed, a whirlpool in the bathroom, a small sitting room with a full-size TV, and fresh flowers. Everything you want and need is luxuriously at your fingertips.

These refinements of course make traveling more enjoyable, but it also means that you need to be more realistic as you plan. These creature comforts and accommodations are not inexpensive, and to take the kind of trip that you want and need, you'll need a lot of money set aside.

CHALLENGES OF TRAVEL

Though travel is a wonderful, incomparable experience, engaging, planning, and executing travel itineraries is not always easy. You must select destinations, weigh options, consider costs, accept risks, and seek consensus with other members of the party. Meticulous planning is necessary if you are to avoid mistakes. Many things must be determined before you even walk out the door, such as:

- Airline schedules, ticketing, layovers, baggage allowances, luggage transfer, and connecting flights

- Hotel reservations, room rates, convenience, and quality of room accommodations

- Car rentals (or servicing your own car), maps, current driver's license, tour bus tickets, river cruises, and rail passes

- Tickets for stage shows, museums, and athletic events, plus dining reservations

- A wardrobe tailored to seasonal change and a schedule that factors in jet lag due to time-zone changes

- Prescription medications, health insurance cards, immunizations, and prophylactic medicine such as a broad-spectrum antibiotics

- Adequate American and foreign currency, plus two widely accepted credit cards

- Passports, birth certificates, and visas

- Arrangements for the dog and cat, plus home surveillance, mail collection, snow removal, temporary cancellation of subscriptions, and the removal of newspapers and extraneous papers

- Review of foreign cultures and languages

In particular, every foreign destination has challenges for the tourist. You must be acquainted with the currency exchange rates, hotels, transportation, and security issues of a different country. Foreign shores also eliminate many of the reminders of home. Differing time zones, unfamiliar phone systems, language barriers, quirky electric converters, outrageous phone bills, and week-old copies of the *New York Times* and *Wall Street Journal* conspire to shut the door on the information you typically follow day-to-day at home.

You must be acquainted with the currency exchange rates, hotels, transportation, and security issues of a different country.

However, the Internet has gone a long way toward overcoming much of this disconnect. Most, if not all, modern hotels offer Internet connections, and most towns across the world have Internet. A laptop is very handy to travel with, particularly if you wish to communicate by email and access news about current events. Crayon.net and ecola.com are websites through which you can read virtually any newspaper throughout the world.

Frequent travelers seem to delight in cataloging their stressful experiences while traveling abroad. Be it poor service, inconvenience, getting lost, becoming ill, or distress of any kind, there is a fascination with retelling minor misadventures. Why are the bumps along the road the most memorable? Perhaps a bad-luck story or a tale of overcoming adversity is of greater interest to the listener, while at the same time providing bragging rights to the survivor. A taxi ride in Rome or rude treatment at a French restaurant make for good stories. Travel miscues can produce highly comical situations.

The seasoned traveler has come to expect a certain degree of organized chaos, impromptu glitches, and aggravating delays when going on a foreign junket. Travel is moody and unpredictable; it swings like a pendulum between hurry up and wait, run and sit, rigid schedule and improvisation. This undulation, however disconcerting, often creates a sense of comic relief and resignation, and the tribulations of travel, if creatively recorded in a travel diary, become a literary comedy to be enjoyed for years to come.

> *The seasoned traveler has come to expect a certain degree of organized chaos.*

Itineraries today offer an infinite number of travel options. If you traveled twelve months a year, you could visit just a small percentage of the outstanding destinations that dot all corners of the globe. There is always a unique hideaway and adventure awaiting your arrival.

Demands of Travel

Travel is stressful. It introduces you to new surroundings where everything is a little, or a lot, different. Because nothing resembles home, you must pay attention, since the subconscious autopilot that guides your activities at home will lead you off course in unfamiliar surroundings. Overloaded by the fatigue of travel, you must still remember new instructions. Each travel destination has its own set of ground rules. If you are checking into a hotel, what is the procedure for parking your rental car, and whom do you tip? Who will take care of your luggage, and how do you secure your valuables and passports? Where is the dining room and bar, and when do they open? What are the cable TV channels? How do you adjust the room temperature?

The shape you are in and amount of time you want to spend preparing must play a role in your travel decisions.

Many more mundane questions need answers. You must orchestrate your plans to meet friends, keep up with the tour activities, buy tickets to shows and tourist attractions, make reservations for dining, plan your exercise routine, and arrange for a wake-up call. Living out of a suitcase, tolerating crumpled clothes, and repeated packing are other challenges. Taken individually, each item is fairly ordinary, but taken together in the context of unfamiliar settings, they are tedious and wearing. Before you plan a big trip, make sure you are physically and mentally up to the challenges and stress. The shape you are in and amount of time you want to spend preparing must play a role in your travel decisions.

VISITING FAMILY AND CLOSE FRIENDS

Visits to the homes of family members and close friends require a greater emotional adjustment than a standard tour. You are rarely as relaxed in someone else's home as you are in your own home. Sleepovers especially complicate a visit. Generally, when you sleep over, your schedule becomes the schedule of the person you visit. And each private residence is different. You must be prepared for a foldaway bed with steel ribs or a double bed for two adults that slopes toward the center. Unlike a hotel, the refinements and protocols in a private residence do not conform to any standard. Within every home resides a unique family culture and unique individuals who exhibit a wide variety of personality traits.

Just like with major holidays or vacations, anticipation and expectations build as you plan visits to friends and relatives. After you arrive, the meticulous planning, expense, and effort that you have put into the visit produces a feeling of entitlement. You count on the friendship and fond memories from the past to erupt into an atmosphere of conviviality and intimacy. But all relationships carry a mixture of feelings, and time changes our personalities and circumstances. As a result, these visits often disappoint.

But all relationships carry a mixture of feelings, and time changes our personalities and circumstances.

However, visiting with friends is a joyous part of travel. The key to avoiding unrealistic expectations is to lower them. Graciously accept what is offered, and realize that long visits often intrude on the host's normal routines. Try to avoid the unwanted overdose of closeness that can result in tacit closing remarks like, "I couldn't wait to get out of there and get back home," and "I thought they were never going to leave."

FOREIGN TRAVEL

Travel outside the United States adds complexity and additional requirements to the planning and execution. You need a passport, inoculations against infectious diseases endemic to the region where you're headed, and greater organization and structure to your travel plans to avoid problems. Language barriers are probably the most difficult obstacle and must be factored into travel plans. Exposure to contagious diseases due to poor sanitation is a legitimate threat that must be weighed country by country. More recently, security concerns related to political unrest and terrorism have become the paramount consideration in scheduling overseas adventures, especially to the Middle East and other areas where Islamic fundamentalism has a presence. To gather information about travel advisories and warnings, search the Internet or check with the American embassy services.

Tourists are becoming more welcome and even necessary all over the world.

Moreover, Americans are envied in some foreign countries because of the high standard of living; also, anti-American sentiment due to unpopular foreign policies can be found all over the world. The brash "ugly American" label is still widely applied to the American tourist across Europe and Asia, where subtlety and greater caution are hallmarks of the cultures. These prejudices can translate into miscommunication and indifferent service.

However, as Americans, Japanese, Chinese, Indians, and Germans and other Europeans are making travel junkets to all corners of the globe, tourists are becoming more welcome and even necessary all over the world. Their tourist dollars, yen, yuan, rupees, and euros have transformed the Earth into a variegate cornucopia of superb travel destinations. English is widely taught and is becoming the universal second language. To capture tourist dollars, most governments strive to welcome visitors and make travel safe and comfortable. And most countries have magnificent natural attractions, museums, restaurants, and more that will be more than happy to have you.

Jet Lag

Aside from gastrointestinal complaints, jet lag is the most troublesome disorder associated with overseas travel. It warrants individual discussion because it consistently detracts from the experience on both ends of the journey. Jet lag is the excessive daytime sleepiness, mild disorientation, and insomnia that occur with travel across multiple time zones. In medical terms, it produces an alteration in the sleep-wake cycle and the circadian rhythms that develop due to daylight and darkness. The severity of jet lag depends upon the number of time zones crossed, the direction of travel, your age, and individual differences in making the adjustment.

Normal sleep patterns change dramatically with age. In older individuals, sleep studies reveal a reduction in deep sleep, frequent spontaneous wakening, and an inability to sleep in. These age-related differences make recovery from jet lag a greater problem for the older traveler. Most travelers experience more difficulty with sleep problems when traveling west to east than east to west. Traveling from winter to summer, such as to the southern hemisphere or to a tropical country in November or December, seems to cause less jet lag. The return trip, however, produces the reverse seasonal effect. The longer the stay, the longer it takes to readjust when returning home. A rule of thumb is one day for each time zone difference.

Steps can be taken to minimize and abbreviate jet lag. Stay hydrated by drinking water, and avoid taking any stimulants such as alcoholic beverages or caffeine. Melatonin is a naturally occurring hormone secreted by a small gland in the brain called the pineal gland. This hormone influences sleep patterns, and a high amount causes drowsiness. Melatonin is widely available without a prescription. Low doses taken thirty minutes before bedtime for the three or four days at the beginning and ending of a trip help to accelerate the readjustment to the time-zone change. In the pharmaceutical pipeline there are several additional medications that are derivatives of melatonin. In recent clinical trials these appear to be safe, effective, and nonaddictive.

A rule of thumb is one day for each time zone difference.

Likewise there are some newer sleeping medications such as Ambien and Sonata that quickly induce sleep, are rapidly excreted by the body, and produce little or no medicinal hangover. Taking one of these medications on a temporary basis under the advice of your physician may help to more quickly reestablish your normal sleep pattern.

COST CONSIDERATIONS

Travel can be expensive, especially if you wish to travel first class during the height of the tourist season or go to world-class resorts, especially when the value of the American dollar is plummeting. To minimize costs, globe-trotters are well advised to search major travel sites on the Web such as Travelocity, Expedia, and Orbitz for bargains on discounted airfares, special travel packages, and new resort promotions. Frequently, when the airlines are competing to carve out a greater market share in select destinations, fares become unbelievably low. But to qualify for many deeply discounted airfares, you must travel during low-volume periods, depart from smaller airports other than main hubs, and choose destinations where airlines are trying to squeeze out a smaller carrier.

Travel agencies also have access to excellent travel deals. Their computer systems can scan around the world for attractive travel packages in price ranges that suit almost any budget. Moreover, the agent's experience and depth of travel knowledge provides enormous value to the customer. Especially when traveling overseas, their practical advice and coaching can help customize a travel package that circumvents risks and inconvenience. There is little or no added cost to book through a travel agent, since their fees are derived from a percentage rebate from the vendors.

Membership in the American Automobile Association (AAA) costs around $100 per year for a family and provides a broad range of benefits for both travelers and non-travelers. Membership provides timely highway service by certified agents at discounted prices. Discounts at many hotel chains and other establishments are offered to cardholders. AAA provides free travel booklets for each region of the United States that list and rate lodging and dining facilities. In thousands of offices nationwide, they provide free road maps and TripTiks.

Recent geopolitical concerns have had a profound impact on the travel market. Indeed, in countries affected by terrorism, there are many genuine travel bargains, and much of this deeply discounted travel is available in countries that are relatively safe and avoided by tourists only because they are adjacent to regions plagued by terrorism.

Even with discounted travel arrangements, a steady diet of travel is expensive. Discounted travel packages often include just the basics of travel and lodging with few frills. Activities such as playing the slot machines, deep-sea fishing, scuba diving, sailing, gourmet dining, sporting events, stage shows, spa services, cooking classes, side trips, golf, tennis, horseback riding, trap shooting, and so on quickly add up. State and local taxes must also be tacked onto the bill. At the end of the stay, when the bill is paid and you are leaving to go home, a sense of buyer's regret frequently settles in.

Even with discounted travel arrangements, a steady diet of travel is expensive.

Time spent away detracts from time at home. This is especially true for seasonal migrants from the North to the South, or snowbirds who spend the three to six colder months in places like Florida or Arizona. Long periods away interfere with the home routine. You must enlist replacements for your poker, bridge, tennis, bowling, and golf groups. Many social events such as graduations, weddings, anniversaries, christenings, professional meetings, parties, holiday celebrations, and funerals are missed. Your home still must be heated, the gutters cleaned, the houseplants watered, and the lawn cared for. Provisions to pay routine bills, check the house, tend to the pet, open important mail, and cancel paper delivery must be made. There are always many small loose ends to tie together when traveling away for extended periods.

Select a destination with modern facilities that are tailored to serve the tourist industry.

All of these things must be taken together to determine the real cost of your travel. Make sure you map out a budget before you begin planning that accounts for both what you will spend on the trip and what you will need to spend to take care of your home while you are gone.

IMPROVING THE TRAVEL EXPERIENCE

Travel advertisements and brochures flood the print media you read, your email, and your mailbox. Travel books and websites abound with special packages, and an infinite array of invitations to join tour groups comes from all directions—friends, professional societies, universities, museums, historical societies, special interest groups, hobby enthusiasts, and tour agencies.

Just a few words of advice: Unless you are a rugged backpacker or renounce the amenities of home, select a destination with modern facilities that are tailored to serve the tourist industry. Although it makes for an interesting travel escapade to go to the most remote corner of the globe with primitive tribes, Third World facilities, rutted dirt roads, and *Survivor*-like challenges, there are few who sign up a second time. Poor hygienic conditions can expose you to bacteria like toxic E. coli that causes the Montezuma's revenge of fever and diarrhea. The poor sanitary conditions within the developing world increase the risk of infectious disease such as amebiasis, hepatitis, malaria, giardiasis, and even septic bacterial infections. If there are any questions about sanitation, it is generally best to drink bottled water without ice and eat in restaurants recommended for tourists. In the Third World, it is inadvisable to eat in the local marketplace.

Carry a supply of a broad-spectrum antibiotics for general use in treating garden-variety respiratory, gastroenteric, or urinary tract infection.

Since the quality of bed pillows varies greatly, you might consider packing a compressible down pillow in your suitcase. Important prescription medications should be hand-carried to avoid loss, since replacement is next to impossible in most foreign countries. Carry a supply of a broad-spectrum antibiotics for general use in treating garden-variety respiratory, gastroenteric, or urinary tract infection. When you have your medical checkup to make sure you are fit for the journey, your physician, if asked, will probably give you a prescription or some antibiotics samples.

Actual travel time is usually composed of 5 percent hurry up and 95 percent wait. Take along your iPod and good reading material to pass the time. Being confined to a seat with few options to keep you amused makes reading more pleasurable.

The recent medical literature links the development of blood clots in the leg (phlebothrombosis) and pulmonary embolus with sitting in one position for long periods during extended flights. Therefore, it is advisable to get up and walk around the cabin periodically to prevent this from happening. If you have a history of severe varicose veins or lower-extremity deep venous thrombosis, you should consider wearing compression hose and taking more frequent trips up and down the aisles.

HOME SWEET HOME

Most love the anticipation and change of scenery that are a part of traveling. But no matter how invigorating a trip might be, returning home always brings a warm sense of anticipation. As trite as it may seem, home is where the heart resides. You know the territory, and the familiarity is reassuring. At home you control the definition of comfort. Your home offers some accoutrements that invariably elude distant havens. Some of the favorites are a complete wardrobe to choose from, a full-sized refrigerator to raid, a car waiting to drive, a hometown newspaper to read, old friends to greet, and a mattress that perfectly conforms to your body.

Returning home always brings a warm sense of anticipation.

Travel is designed for retirees who like the challenge of managing the travel experience. It produces adventure and intellectual stimulation and is a clear break from routine. Plan well, budget wisely, and then enjoy.

CHAPTER 24

Working in Retirement

A full-time job is a full-time commitment, and few workers have the luxury to just coast and be happily underemployed during the final years of their careers. A staggered disengagement and semiretired status are uncommon words in the business vernacular.

In strategic business plans, retention and development of older employees is rarely mentioned. Discussions about retirees primarily surface when the company is reviewing pension-fund obligations and health benefits that impact their income statements and balance sheets. Many companies raise their estimated rates of return (hurtle rate) on retirement accounts to lower their funding obligations and improve the bottom line. This invitation to gross under-funding coupled with poor stock performance has put the pension plans of many major corporations in serious jeopardy. Also, for pension plans that are richly funded or even contain a surplus, this has justified corporate raiding of these plans with little to no regard for the employees it will affect.

There are broad pressures for senior workers to retire with the vitality tank still half full.

Few businesses have written plans that support a kind and gentle downward slope to transition workers into retirement—in fact, lowering budget expenditures often comes down to forcing out higher-paid and older employees. With increasing age comes a rising company liability for health care, deferred compensation, and training to master new technology. Many companies craft retirement packages filled with incentives that propel and subtly coerce the executives and managers into early retirement. Regardless of the provisions within the Age Discrimination in Employment Act of 1967, at the end of the day, there are broad pressures for senior workers to retire with the vitality tank still half full.

> *Fully one third of men and women take up new or part-time jobs within a year of retirement.*

The American blueprint for career pathways usually shows a steady progression up the corporate ladder with an abrupt stop at the top rung. Unfortunately, there usually is no blueprint showing the descent down the ladder. American society would benefit if similar weight were placed on both the ascent and descent on this figurative ladder. And it would go a long way toward solving the demographic shift in age that inexorably will challenge public policy during the twenty-first century.

Fully one third of men and women take up new or part-time jobs within a year of retirement. Both employers and employees would benefit if these workers stayed on as part-time workers with the same parent firms.

VOLUNTEER WORK

A high proportion of Americans perform volunteer services. Today, the American economy benefits from the work of 65–70 million volunteers, and the nonprofit sector accounts for a hefty 12 percent of America's GDP. There are approximately 1.5 million tax-exempt organizations registered with the Internal Revenue Service and 350,000 religious organizations that are not required to register with the IRS.

Nonprofits are generally considered providers of charity care and the "social safety net" of last resort. These organizations have traditionally filled the gaps in social services that are unmet by the government. And these gaps have increased in recent years as the government has made cutbacks in social welfare and other programs.

The diversity of nonprofit organizations is amazing. The National Taxonomy of Exempt Entities (NTEE) divides them into ten major categories, twenty-six groups, and over six hundred subgroups. The major categories are arts, culture and humanities, education, environment and animals, health, human services, international and foreign affairs, public, societal benefit, religion-related, mutual membership benefit, and unknown organizations. Each category has different affiliated organizations, dependence upon the various sources of revenue, use of volunteers, concentrations of resources, stated missions and goals, and approaches to social entrepreneurship. The size and prominence of individual organizations within each category also varies widely.

The diversity of nonprofit organizations is amazing.

Getting Started

Retirees contribute more hours to volunteer service than any other group of people. Some organizations, such as religious and relief agencies, view dedicated volunteers as indispensable to their operations. The fine arts depend heavily upon volunteers for staffing, fund-raising, committee work, and boards of governance. Some agencies such as Habitat for Humanity use the skills of senior craftsmen to build low-income housing, and the Senior Corps of Retired Executives (SCORE) uses experienced executives as counselors to America's small businesses.

Volunteerism has many intangible benefits. It allows you to interact with like-minded people who have a shared purpose. Volunteers are caring people drawn from all age groups with a rich cross-section of diversity and work experience; it's a good way to make new friends and establish a broader network of acquaintances. Volunteer work is a way to stay active while still being in control of your time commitment. You have the option to select volunteer work that meets your needs, addresses your passion, and matches your skills. And you'll feel good about lending a helping hand.

Volunteers are often recruited via word of mouth within the community, though you can find many websites, such as the Points of Light Foundation (www.pointsoflight.org), that are excellent ways to start your search for suitable volunteer opportunities. However, the best way to begin is to define your area of interest and see what activities mesh with your retirement mission statement.

You can find a general listing of local volunteer agencies under "Social Service Organizations" in the phone book. For more specific services, such as child adoption or home health care, you would look under those headings. A simple telephone call to almost any charitable agency usually produces a wealth of information, and a live representative will send you brochures, applications, and additional information. This congenial response reflects the "service to humanity" mantra that characterizes the not-for-profit sector. Moreover, the local director of the agency and volunteer program is usually actively involved in public relations and volunteer recruitment—a request to meet with the director is often considered routine.

In recent times, scams and accounting scandals have shaken the nonprofit sector. In response, the sector now espouses the principle that tax-exempt enterprises should be managed with the same transparency and generally accepted accounting standards as firms in the for-profit sector. Volunteer programs and the volunteers themselves should also be managed with the same due diligence as regular hourly workers. Many talented individuals have become disenchanted with volunteer programs because they often are loosely administered and wasteful of their skills. When looking for an organization to give your time to, it is wise to put the prospective agency under the magnifying glass. Ask questions, and use some of the following criteria to make a value judgment about the volunteer opportunity and whether you would enjoy being a part of it.

Organizational Structure

- How transparent are the organization's finances, and can you view this data? What services do the donations and service revenues support? What is the expense ratio between fund-raising and administrative costs versus dollars actually spent on services to carry out the mission?

- Does the volunteer program have a full-time director who coordinates and is accountable for its success? Through what activities does the director maintain a close working relation-ship with the volunteers? After your initial interview, what are your impressions of the director? To whom does the di-rector report?

- Does the volunteer program afford an opportunity to advance into positions of greater responsibility such as administrative duties, committee assignments, and super-visory roles? Conversely, if you are an outstanding volun-teer, how will you resist becoming more involved than you originally planned?

- Who benefits from your efforts—the national, regional, or local agencies within the parent organization? What tangible effects does it have on your community?

- Does the volunteer program have a budget?

- What is involved in the interviewing and application process, and how are volunteers oriented and assigned positions?

Policy

- Is there a manual of standard operating procedures and protocol?

- What activities and functions does the organization assign to the volunteer? Are volunteers given equal status and respect, as if they were paid staff, or are they viewed mainly as donors, fund-raisers, or public relations contacts?

- Do the volunteers have "job descriptions," and how empowered are they to make decisions?

- What educational credentials and work experience are required?

- How does the agency reward and recognize its volunteers?

- Is there a process to voice grievances? Does the director meet with the volunteer on a regular basis to exchange ideas and deal with problems?

- Do any of the volunteers get paid?

Day-to-Day Details

- How many hours are you expected to work per week, and how flexible is the schedule and time commitment? Is it a seasonal or annual activity only?

- How is training provided? What are the opportunities for learning and on-the-job-training?

- Is there a range of activities to offer variety?

- How safe is the area in which you will be working? Do you have to go occasionally into high-crime areas within the city? Is parking a problem, and how much does it cost?

- What kind of people will you be working with, and what are the opportunities to make new friends?

- What is the volunteer turnover rate per year?

- How are volunteers viewed by the regular, paid staff?

This list reflects a range of human-resource issues that may seem like things you would worry about in a job and not in volunteer work. However, volunteers are representatives and agents of non-profits in addition to providing services for them, and as such they deserve the same attention as regular employees.

Retirees are a treasure trove of experience and skills, well positioned to shoulder a large share of the glaring needs within our communities. Volunteer work can be attractive and rewarding, replete with a mission and new use of your old skills. Volunteers with passion are uniquely positioned to advance the goals of the charities they serve.

MENTORING

Mentoring is a more focused form of volunteer work. A mentor is usually a role model and trusted counselor to an individual or group who helps spur development or create achievement goals. Mentors have close personal contact with the organizations or people they help. Retirees, who bring to the table a flexible schedule and knowledge and empathy amassed over many years of experience, tend to be some of the very best mentors.

Mentoring activities fall into many classifications. Schools use Big Brother mentors to offer remedial training to young people, while family agencies use them to assist in behavior modification within families. Law enforcement agencies use mentors as guidance resources for troubled juveniles. Businesses use them for succession training, and in the creative arts, mentors train docents and potential board candidates. There is a wide spectrum of purposeful activity that these coaches and confidants employ to better our communities. Below are some of the goals and objectives common to mentoring programs.

Goals

Identify areas for growth and development.
Provide specific skill training.
Listen to and evaluate situational problems.
Explore options and risk-taking to solve dilemmas.
Review and communicate educational needs.
Provide appropriate and timely advice.
Confront negative intentions and behaviors.
Identify and support latent talents.

Emotional Transitional Goals

Immature to mature behavior
Destructive to constructive behavior
Dependence to independence
Hopelessness to options

Getting Started

Most mentoring programs accept differing levels of participation that match the availability and expertise of the mentor with the needs of the program. As with other forms of volunteer opportunities, there are no centralized registries that post available positions. Recruitment is usually word of mouth. But the need for mentors is great, and there are many opportunities, both within formalized programs and in your own backyard.

Most mentoring programs accept differing levels of participation that match the availability and expertise of the mentor with the needs of the program.

Mentoring and assisting in schools deserves special mention. Public schools were created to focus solely on education. They were not institutions designed to counteract negative behaviors and act as disciplinary policemen. But today there is a growing number of children who do not get the care they need at home, and educational systems have been forced to provide physical security as well as requirements that should be met at home, such as feeding and sheltering. Teenage pregnancy, child abuse, and abandonment all pass the duty of raising children onto the schools. The needs in our schools are overwhelming, and a mentor can make a real difference.

Most retirees have not visited a K-12 inner-city school for many years; I encourage you to do so. If you express an interest in mentoring activities, the principal, teachers, and counselors will seize on this and quickly provide ideas on how you can become involved in this important work. Depending on the school, here are some of the places where you might be needed:

- Volunteer as a librarian's assistant, and mentor kids about the importance of reading.

- Become a member of the school alumni society, and mentor junior and senior students toward graduation and higher education.

- Help institute or run programs that coordinate efforts to bring parents and teachers together to share responsibility for their children's education.

- Meet weekly with an underachieving youngster to offer advice, encouragement, and assistance in reading, writing, and arithmetic.

- Teach values and winning behaviors in the elementary schools.

- Become a scout leader.

- Coach a Little League team.

- Participate in the youth programs supported by Rotary, Lions, and Kiwanis clubs.

- Volunteer at an after-school activity center.

Compassionate mentoring may be the very best way to make a tangible investment in our nation's future and give back to the community. Mentoring is a way to care for the children and businesses in your area, and your unique skills and job and life experience can really make a difference in their success.

COMMUNITY SERVICE

The term "community service" might make you think of a court sentence, but in a larger sense, community service is relevant to all retirees interested in giving back to the community. This thoughtful blend of mentoring and volunteering in most instances matches your qualifications and capabilities with the needs in your own backyard and neighborhood. Following are some ways that you can offer valuable services to your community—do any of them fit with your retirement plans?

Teaching

- Volunteer with a golf, tennis, soccer, bowling, or debate team within a local school.

- Assist the local actors' guild or high-school thespian society with their live theater productions.

- Sponsor and help with middle-school or high-school extra-curricular activities such as a math, physics, chess, travel, stock investing, 4-H, or computer club.

- Volunteer to visit schools and teach manners, morality, safety, relationships, constructive behaviors, and good hygiene to grade-school children in the classroom.

- Teach a course about a subject in which you are an expert at a local college or trade school.

- Join a community service organization that sponsors scholarship and youth development programs.

- Host a fund-raiser for a special-education program, and visit with the kids served by the program.

- Act as a crossing guard, or volunteer to be a class assistant.

Community Administration

- Serve on the local school board, or be active in the PTA and other organizations that help facilitate communication between teachers, parents, and the community.

- Offer to serve on the village council, zoning commission, or architectural review board.

- Assist the volunteer fire department and emergency squads in their outreach and safety programs.

- Seek to help the local historical/preservation society in their research efforts, and offer administrative help.

- Be an assistant librarian, or provide a free tax service at the community center.

- If qualified, do accounting work and provide consulting services to local government, churches, and charitable organizations.

- Be active in the local senior citizens' group and its programs to help homebound and handicapped people.

Environmental

- Join the garden club and get involved with community beautification projects.

- Support preservation organizations that protect our rivers, natural resources, and architectural heritage.

- Sponsor and participate in neighborhood cleanup programs.

These are just a few of the many, many ways in which you can perform community service that will both put your job skills to the test and help other people in your area. Creativity, effort, and donations can make a huge difference.

MORE ON HOBBIES

Those planning retirement often think that they have too few hobbies and outside pursuits to fill their newfound surplus of time. And this may be a realistic fear, since most individuals with careers in progress have not had the time to seriously dig into avocations, hobbies, and other sidelined pastimes. Hobbies can consume as much or as little time as you wish to give them. Pastimes such as woodworking, needlework, puzzle making, and model railroading are examples in which the time commitment is perfectly discretionary. Moreover, you work at your own speed, without supervision, and only when you want to. Hobbies can be extremely relaxing and pleasant activities.

Most individuals with careers in progress have not had the time to seriously dig into avocations, hobbies, and other sidelined pastimes.

The process to pursue a new hobby is fairly simple. Pick something you understand and are enthusiastic about. Follow this with some basic research, and, as a part of your filtering process, answer some of the following basic questions:

- How much will it cost?

- What are the time requirements?

- What physical and mental effort will be required?

- Do I have the dexterity to become proficient?

- How much additional learning is required?

- What potential social value does it produce?

- What is the resale or investment value to a collection?

- Are there travel opportunities?

- Is it a solo or group activity?

Figure out which of these attributes are important to you, then explore a few hobbies that satisfy your requirements. Make sure you try a few—this is a good way to happen upon one that is both fulfilling and fun.

The Joy of Stamp Collecting

Stamp collection is a good illustration of all hobbying. To help beginners get started, most philatelic or stamp-collecting societies have websites that provide basic information. They offer introductory materials and advice for beginners, as well as benchmarks and guidelines for evaluating the mint condition of individual stamps and how stamps are traded online and in the marketplace. After surfing these sites, go to the local library and read introductory texts about stamp collecting. Then buy one or more of the more common reference textbooks used by stamp collectors.

Follow this by making the rounds at the local post office and stores where stamps are traded or sold. Look for hobby fairs where stamps are exhibited, and if you attend a trade fair, talk to other collectors and ask for their feelings and impressions about the business and social aspects of stamp collecting. At this point you will have put a face on the discipline of stamp collecting and can make a judgment on whether it meshes with your interests. Then begin to dig deeper. Consider your costs to get started and what your investment budget might be. Contact local philatelic clubs and attend some of their meetings. Refine your interest by deciding if you want to specialize in stamps from a single nation, region, or era. Find information about educational seminars relevant to your hobby, and contact the national philatelic societies to see if they offer correspondence courses that fulfill certification requirements. Talk up your hobby with friends and grandchildren.

Consider your costs to get started and what your investment budget might be.

After you have done your homework and become knowledgeable in your new hobby, you gain the respect of other collectors and have a clearer perspective of the market. It probably will take just three to five years to become an expert, well positioned to trade with the professionals. From your efforts a fine collection of stamps may emerge, not to mention a small side business that supplements your fixed income. And your investment probably will appreciate, act as a hedge against inflation, and be enthusiastically received by the rest of the family.

Stamp collecting may seem old-fashioned and even a little boring, but I have seen stamp collectors with as much passion for their hobby as any model train collector, vegetable gardener, alpine hiker, and anthropological digger. Franklin Roosevelt was a noted philatelist.

Valuable Collections

In recent years, many collections have become highly desirable in the tangibles market and command outrageous prices at auction. Almost anything that is a limited edition or very rare, even if it dates back only to the middle of the nineteenth century, brings premium prices. For instance, who could have ever imagined that the baseball trading cards we played with as kids would become so valuable?

In view of the dramatic increase in the value of many unusual things—antique toys, cone-top beer cans, campaign buttons, authentic Navaho Indian jewelry, Persian rugs, movie posters, dollhouses, classic automobiles, war relics, pottery, and much more—one frequently wonders what trendy items will bring the next windfall to the collector. For the investor, prices in the equity markets and real estate may seem unpredictable and volatile, but at least valuations are based on fundamentals; in the tangibles market, perception and the eye of the beholder rule. So if you have any old collections, as strange and worthless as they may seem, it might be a good idea to hang onto them. You never know when the market will shift its focus, and its gaze might come to rest upon one of the piles in your garage.

Birdwatching

Birdwatching or "birding" is one of the fastest growing outdoor activities in America. The U.S. Fish and Wildlife Service estimates the number of serious hobbyists at 46 million. Bird lovers spend roughly $34 billion a year on bird feeders, birdseed, binoculars, field guides, travel, and specialty clothing such as gumboots, anoraks, and wooly hats. The most intense birdwatchers, known as "twitchers," are enthusiasts who pursue rare species to build lists of sightings and bird study. Birdwatching is a very relaxing and enjoyable hobby: It soothes the psyche, carries a bargain price, fits into any schedule constraint, requires little prior training, and promotes a healthy, active lifestyle.

Sports

For some retirees, sports and sporting events are the preferred activities of retirement. Golf, tennis, walking, swimming, horseback riding, sailing, and many other sports can help to quickly repopulate an open schedule. Participation in athletics is especially well suited if you have been a sports enthusiast over the years and have basic proficiency in a range of physical activities. Most non-contact sports are timeless and can be enjoyed into advanced age. Certainly anyone who can shoot their age in golf has legitimate bragging rights.

Golf seems to be the most popular sport amongst retirees. But one caveat is warranted: Taking up golf as a brand-new activity without prior experience can be aggravating and frustrating. This is especially true if you wish to play with an avid, serious group of golfers. Golf was defined by Mark Twain as "a good walk spoiled" for a reason. However, if you have the objectivity to not care a stitch about your score and handicap, if you play with others who are equally inept, if you avoid heavy betting, and if you compete only with yourself, golf is a great and relaxing pastime.

Anyone who can shoot their age in golf has legitimate bragging rights.

When deciding to venture into a new sport, ask some of the following questions:

- What is the learning curve and frustration quotient to become proficient?

- Are the costs reasonable and affordable?

- How much time and preparation are required?

- Do you have a circle of friends with whom to share the activity?

- Can your physique handle the exertion?

- How enjoyable is the sport, and do you enjoy the company of the people with whom you will be playing?

- What are the social opportunities attached to the sport?

- Will the sport aggravate any previous orthopedic injuries, and what are the risks of new injury?

- Is the sport an aerobic sport—will it stimulate your endorphin levels, control your weight, and improve your physical conditioning?

- When you observe others playing the sport, do they smile and laugh a lot?

- Can it be shared with children and grandchildren?

Physical fitness is an imperative for health and happiness, and athletic activities are an enjoyable way to make it happen.

Games

Adults often play some card and board games, but unless they become a social routine with a regular bridge, chess, or backgammon group, games really aren't that important to them. However, for retirees, the old mind-enhancing games such as bridge, chess, Scrabble, Monopoly, and backgammon can be a source of stimulation and polite social interaction. Social gatherings often revolve around a game venue, and most groups are looking for new players to join. Likewise, many clinics and introductory programs are available to help a player learn and perfect his or her game. Playing board games and cards usually transcends age and gender differences, and it's a leisurely way to socialize and make new friends on a level playing field—chance and luck, instead of skill and experience, tend to determine the outcome, making it fun for everyone.

Also, it's interesting to note that doctors and therapists have begun recommending the video game system Nintendo Wii for people who have difficulties exercising or with hand-eye coordination. If you have limited mobility, this can be a great and fun way to stay in shape. And your grandkids will love to come over and play it with you!

Epilogue

In 1967 Congress passed the Age Discrimination in Employment Act (ADEA), which protects people between the ages of forty and sixty-five from job discrimination because of their age. In 1986 the act was amended to prohibit mandatory retirement ages (with a few exceptions).

Regardless of this explicit legislation, there remains widespread cultural age discrimination in American life. This highlights the need for significant social change—the steadily increasing talent pool of seniors may soon need to be drawn into the mainstream of corporate America. And no matter what happens, corporate America needs to be kinder, gentler, and more accommodating to the aging worker.

To start with, more social research is warranted to better understand the issues and offer solutions to this expanding gray wave. Few, if any, universities have programs that are focused on retirees. Why not establish major departments dedicated to retirement studies, senior resources, second career options, and new directions? It seems reasonable that integrated programs for senior studies could bring together the disciplines of anthropology, sociology, psychology, physiology, social policy, ethics, and business that relate to the retirement experience. These initiatives could form the basis for programs designed to lengthen the productive working experience plus teach retirees the art of retirement and how to embrace greater self-direction, self-sufficiency, and self-satisfaction.

Readings on Human Sexuality

Barback, Lonnie G. *For Yourself: The Fulfillment of Female Sexuality.* New York: Signet, 2000.

Brown, Helen G. *Sex and the Single Girl.* New York: Barricade Books, 2003.

Chapman, Gary D. *The Five Love Languages: How to Express Heartfelt Commitment to Your Mate.* Chicago: Northfield Publishing, 2003.

Comfort, Alex. *The Joy of Sex.* London: Octopus Publishing Group, 2002.

Masters, William, and Virginia Johnson. *Human Sexuality.* New York: Lippincott Williamson & Wilkens, 1966.

McCarthy, Barry, and Emily McCarthy. *Rekindling Desire: A Step-by-Step Program to Help Low-Sex and No-Sex Marriages.* New York: Brunner-Routeledge, 2003.

O'Connor, Dagmar. *How to Make Love to the Same Person for the Rest of Your Life and Still Love It.* New York: Doubleday, 1985.

Schover, Leslie R. *Sexuality and Fertility after Cancer.* New York: John Wiley, 1990.

★ APPENDIX B ★
A Bibliography for Smart Investing

Dreman, David. *Contrarian Investment Strategies.* New York: Simon & Schuster, 1998.

Graham, Benjamin, with Jason Zweig. *The Intelligent Investor,* revised ed. New York: Harper Collins, 1997.

Lynch, Peter, *One Up on Wall Street.* New York: Simon & Schuster, 1989.

Morris, Kenneth M., and Alan M. Spiegel. *The Wall Street Journal Guide to Understanding Money and Investing.* New York: Simon & Schuster, 1999.

Stanley, Thomas J., and William D. Danko. *The Millionaire Next Door: The Surprising Secrets of America's Wealthy.* New York: Simon & Schuster, 1998.

Index

About the Author

Richard G. Wendel, MD, MBA, is a graduate of Dartmouth College, the University of Cincinnati Medical School, and the Williams College of Business at Xavier University. He retired in 1997 after thirty-one years practicing medicine.